Enjoy the Ride

"I will be including this book with every baby shower gift I give from here on out! I remember as a new mom feeling overwhelmed with so much new information. I wish I'd had Suzy's book– she speaks to the essentials, giving nuggets of truth spoken in no-nonsense language. As a mom with older children, I wish I had had this book earlier but even after reading it. I immediately put to work some of Suzy's suggestions regarding enjoying mealtime together and it was a hit with my girls!"

-Jana Alayra, *performer of children's music and mother of 3*

"Captivating! I couldn't put it down. As a pre-school teacher for 20 years, I'm excited to finally have a parenting book I can recommend to parents. It's simple, practical, and meaningful; a must for busy parents!"

-Tamara Gallagher, *preschool teacher of 20 years*

"Suzy succinctly writes about many of the issues related to parenting in a relational, practical, and positive manner."

-Susan Peterson, *author of* Fun and Educational Places to Go with Kids and Adults in Southern California *guidebook and mother of 3*

"I highly recommend this book. Suzy has a down-to-earth style dealing with topics important to all parents in a way that's easy-to-read, understand and "put to use."

-Betsy Slauson, *Preschool Director*

"*Enjoy the Ride* is cover-to-cover awesome and has the potential to help any and every parent. Suzy's story-telling approach brings life to the every day joys and challenges of parenthood. Her artful approach to specific strategies and child-rearing techniques is a breath of fresh air. I would have been thrilled to find this information tucked into the hospital bassinet!"

-Judy L. Copenbarger, *attorney, mother of 5, and author of* Teaching our Children about Money

"As a pediatrician, I appreciate Suzy's accurate and straight-forward advice...Suzy's approach to parenting views the child as a 'whole,' addressing not only the physical needs, but also a child's emotional, spiritual, and social needs. *Enjoy the Ride* is concise, user-friendly, and most of all, a true inspiration! It can be finished in one sitting...a must for busy parents!"

-*Tina Wong, M.D., pediatrician and mother of 3*

"I highly recommend this book above all others! Suzy's inspirational words come from years of experience and from a natural instinct for parenting. Anyone who reads this exceptional book will benefit from its advice and tools on the joys and hardships of parenting."

–*J. Arenzana, Educator, Guidance Counselor, and father of 2*

"Not only is *Enjoy the Ride* a pleasure to read, it is also entirely practical and tremendously supportive. My husband and I have appreciated Suzy wise counsel since our son's birth five months ago. Over these past several months we have regularly picked up *Enjoy the Ride* to soak in the useful advice- for example tips on starting solids and suggestions for baby's sleep needs. While reading other parenting books, I have at times felt discouraged and inadequate. In contrast *Enjoy the Ride* leaves me feeling warm and upbeat, as well as empowered and informed. Hooray for realistic and encouraging guidance!"

-*M. Carson, Family therapist and mother of 1*

"It's so unique because it makes me feel like Suzy understands about the emotions involved in parenting. She knows how I feel and how my children might feel. That is unique, refreshing, and inspiring. I've started so many parenting books in my day and not finished, but this book is such an easy-read and something I will refer to over and over again."

-L. Lam, MOPS (Mothers of Preschoolers) leader and mother of 3

"This book offers practical tips that are "right on"; meaning, not just a bunch of lofty, psycho-babble talk. Rather, the author takes you step by step in breaking down how to go about (for example) helping your kids go to bed at night, or how to help them handle their anger, or how to help siblings build up relationships. Good food for thought as well as practical, do-able ideas that will empower any parent!! Parents will finish this quick-read book with a feeling of "Yes, I can do/try that!"

-T. Chan, Elementary school teacher and mother of 4

"Suzy has authority on issues of parenting because of the proof in her children. She is not some pie-in-the-sky theorist but a mom who knows what she's talking about because she's walked the talk and is continuing to do so. Her children are an amazing testimony to her parenting and everyone who meets her and her family would agree."

-M. Tseng, Pastor and adoptive father

What a pleasure to read a book that gives you real life reasonable responses to every day parenting challenges. Suzy gives effective, proven, and loving encouragement. All of it can go beyond 0-10 and into the teen years!!"

-Debby Lewicki, Preschool teacher of 18 years

# Enjoy the Ride

## Tools, Tips, and Inspiration
### for the Most Common Parenting Challenges

## Suzy Martyn

Mother's Friend Publishing
Cypress, CA

*The advice and information in this book are the opinions of the author, and are not intended to replace the care of a licensed medical or psychological practitioner. Please consult the appropriate resources when needed.*

Mother's Friend Publishing
P.O. Box 1020, Cypress, CA 90630.
www.mothersfriendsos.com

Printed in the United States of America.

**Publisher's Cataloging-In-Publication Data**
(Prepared by The Donohue Group, Inc.)

Martyn, Suzy.
  Enjoy the ride : tools, tips, and inspiration for the most common parenting challenges / Suzy Martyn.

  p. : ill. ; cm.

  "Mother's Friend publishing."
  Includes bibliographical references and index.
  ISBN: 978-0-578-00951-3

1. Parenting.  2. Child rearing.  I. Title.

HQ755.8 .M3789 2009
649.1

Mother's Friend
Equip. Support. Inspire. Enjoy!

*To Faith, Grace, and Hope,*
*for the most enjoyable of rides.*


*And to Dave,*
*for buckling into the seat next to me.*

# Contents

## PART THREE: FIVE TO TEN YEARS

# Acknowledgements

This book would have remained in the idea stage if it weren't for the encouragement and support of so many faithful friends who visioned with me, edited chapter after chapter, and kept me focused on the purpose of it all. Thank you Sheri, Wendy, Walene, Laurie, Caroline, Ann, and Becky F.

This book would remain unfinished on my desk if it weren't for the advice and support received from Sue Peterson, Judy Copenbarger, and others who have "gone before."

This book would have had no testing grounds if it weren't for parents like the Dillons, Kams, Crawleys, Arenzanas, and Prewitts, and many others who trusted me with their most precious ones.

This book would have no validity if it weren't for the hours of parenting practice provided by my three amazing daughters: Faith, Grace, and Hope. And thanks to creative "Aunt Glory" and fun "Uncle Bert" for sharing and enjoying the journey together.

This book would remain a disorganized mess if it wasn't for the designing genius of Dave, along with his unending hours of loving support, technical help, parenting partnership, and belief in what I have to offer. And, thank you to Mom and Dad Martyn for raising such a fine son who grew to be such a wonderful daddy for our children!

This book wouldn't be possible if it weren't for the unending support, love, and parenting from the ones who set the precedent: Mimi and Gibi.

This book would be nowhere near publishing if it weren't for the partnership with my bro, Albert. Who knew this little kid was such a business guru? And thank you sister Alice for all the encouragement along the way.

And, finally, this book would be meaningless if it weren't for the amazing purpose God has set before me along with the inspiration to continue to walk through my own journey of parenting. To Him be all the glory.

# Prologue
## All Aboard!

*It's 1:15 p.m. and the temperature outside reads 115 degrees. Three days earlier in our temperate Southern California home, we tuned up, tanked up, wrote up (our itinerary, that is), packed up, and headed out. Now we find ourselves in this hot and dusty desert 200 miles away from home and we're missing that beautiful Southern Californian 75-degree weather. Promises of what lies ahead are not enough to subdue the bickering over imaginary lines in the backseats. Quiet comes only with a promise, threat, or lure of the tube on the road. Ahead lie ghost towns, beaches, parks, playgrounds, mountains, and goldmines, but all we can see is the 700 miles left to go. What happened to that vision of quality, bonding family time and the promise of a time to remember?*

So, are you enjoying the ride?

Remember when you were first thinking about starting a family and you envisioned a quiet, peaceful newborn in your arms as you gazed into her eyes all day long? You dreamt of dressing her up in cute little coordinating outfits, eating bon bons at teahouses together, and living that picture perfect family life.

As the reality of parenting started to set in, what you originally envisioned grew distant in your memory. Lost nights of sleep and regular power struggles with growing children exhausted you and you considered it an accomplishment just to get to the end of the day. You forgot that this was supposed to be fun! Of course, there were good times, but the vision of joy-filled parenting somehow became blurred over time and wear.

That's where this book comes in. Parenting is meant to be enjoyed through and through. Joy is woven in and through even the hardest parts of parenting. The entire package is a miraculous gift wrapped up in the prettiest of packages.

How do I get my children to sleep? Will my baby ever figure out how to breastfeed? How do you set loving limits? Why am I doing all the work around here? All these questions and more are addressed in this book that combines the best of practical how-to in parenting with the inspiration to actually start a new and fresh path today. Once you feel confident and secure about how to handle these type of issues and challenges, there will be less distractions and more space to enjoy parenting as it was intended.

So, buckle up and get ready to recapture that dream of joy in the journey.

# PART ONE

—

# Birth To Two Years

# "Let's Start From the Very Beginning"

## Preparation for Baby

*I'm seven months pregnant with my first child and standing in the baby aisle trying to select items for my baby registry. Part of me is excited at all the cute little fabrics, toys, and ooh, those tiny and irresistible outfits. Excited, yes, but mostly I am overwhelmed and confused. What is an onesie, what kinds of ointment do I need, and how many socks should I scan? I walk to the end of the aisle and turn the corner. I can't believe there's another aisle exclusively devoted to diapers and wipes alone! How can such a little thing need so much?*

## Enjoy the Ride

You are beginning to think about the final preparations before the birth of your baby. Reality is starting to set in. If you haven't yet felt anxious and overwhelmed, you are certainly starting to feel it now. Take a deep breath and know that millions of parents have navigated the road and survived. You will too. Not only that, but it will prove to be a time to mark and remember, trials and all.

One place that can easily cause a parent's pulse to quicken and blood pressure to go up is your local baby superstore. Don't get bogged down with thinking you need every baby item from the start. There are items that you won't need at all or until much later. Of course, you want a new car seat and breast pump for safety reasons, but don't be shy to accept a second-hand cradle or some newborn clothing, especially because they grow out of those as quickly as two weeks! Finally, when it comes down to it, what does a newborn really need besides love, food, diapers, a safe ride in the car, and a warm place to sleep?

If you still feel the need to have a complete list of registry items, (because everything is just so darn cute), then check out my list in the appendix. If I have a particular recommendation for a brand, it's listed. Otherwise, I believe all brands are of equal value and it's really a choice of preference in the features offered.

Aside from having all of the baby equipment ready, take time to talk to your spouse, parents, children and others who will be a part of your growing family. Discuss expectations and areas of concern so that you can be of one mind as you welcome a new member into the family. It could be that your spouse is planning for a large rooting section in the delivery room when you're hoping for a quiet delivery or that your mom is stocking up on different brands of formula when you plan to nurse. Communicating about these things when life is still relatively calm is the best way to go.

In preparation for birth, you will need to make some decisions about how you'd like your experience to be. Even if you feel you know the basics of baby care and childbirth or have already made informed decisions on child birthing options, it is a good idea to attend some classes if only for the purpose of connecting with other new parents and building up a network of support. Many hospitals, colleges, and even maternity stores will offer support groups and classes. Think about classes on child birthing options, infant CPR and first aid, baby care basics, and breastfeeding.

Lastly, and definitely not least, get extra rest. For those first several weeks or longer, it will be somewhat of a commodity! Sneak in naps and long weekend snoozes, especially since pregnancy can have you up and headed for the restroom several times a night. (I think this is nature's way of preparing you for nighttime feedings.)

# 2

# "Bundle of Joy"

## First Days with Baby

When I brought Hope home from the hospital, I explained to her sisters that when a baby wraps her entire little hand around your one finger, that's her way of saying, "I love you." I didn't think this made that much of an impression until one day when 3-year-old Grace was fondly remembering those days with a huge smile on her face. She said, "Mommy? Remember when Hope first started loving us and you said, 'Come here, come here and see how Hope loves you....put your finger in her hand and see how she loves you?'"

## First Night Home

The nurses made it look so easy. Holding them securely with just one hand while bathing them with the other. Perfect swaddles within seconds that lulled baby to sleep. And they always looked so peaceful and calm. The baby *and* the nurses.

It's a different story when you get home and you are on your own. Suddenly you don't know your left from your right and the entire task of caring for a three-day-old baby seems quite foreboding. You thought you knew how to swaddle and you just can't seem to remember if your baby cried this much at the hospital.

Try to remember that just a few short days ago your baby was in a warm, safe place where he never felt discomfort of any kind. He didn't need to breathe, eat, or communicate and now he has to adjust to bright lights, deep breaths, and uncomfortable hunger! Find what works to soothe your baby and take comfort in knowing that this is all just a normal part of the process. Embrace it as a time to get to know your baby, his preferences and personality. I know it's hard to believe now, but even with all the challenges, it's a precious time you will fondly reminisce about as your baby grows.

## What's Normal for a Newborn?

**Crossed eyes** that seem to roll to back of head – When you've just arrived on the scene, even eye muscles need to learn how to work properly. Enjoy glimpses of his gorgeous eyes, however brief they may be, and try not to worry.

**Explosive, wet, yellow and seedy poops** for breastfed babies – Until you see the alternative, you won't appreciate this enough!

**Extra fussiness and inability to settle** and sleep when over-stimulated – Try to limit an over active schedule and balance your time so that your baby has enough down time each day. Calming routines before sleep are invaluable, as well.

**Flaky skin and cradle cap** – You don't need to do anything special to try to remove the skin or cradle cap. All baby's head needs is gentle cleaning with a washcloth and if it makes you feel better, use baby lotion on skin.

**"Infant Puberty"** is around 3 weeks and babies can get acne, eat more, be more awake, and fussy. Sound like a teenager you know? Lotion or cleansers are not necessary. A clean, damp cloth is sufficient. Isn't it ironic that this is also the time you might get your first smile from baby?

**Purple, pink, and blue skin** – A baby's feet can be purple one moment, and then appear pink. As baby's circulation improves, so will her coloring. Blue lips, however, are not normal and need a doctor's evaluation.

**Smiles** from gas that look like "real" smiles and are just enough to touch the heart and bond you to your baby. Fasten your seatbelts. Compared to those amazing belly laughs you're going to see in the next couple months, this is nothing!

**Sneezing, stuffy nose, congestion, and irregular breathing** are normal symptoms for a newborn. In a couple months, nostrils will be bigger and clearer. For now, try some saline drops. Labored breathing, however, (flaring nostrils, extreme chest expansion or grunting) is cause for concern and warrants a call to the pediatrician.

**Straining during bowel movements** does not necessarily mean your baby is constipated. Stools may vary in consistency and color but are most often mustard yellow with a cottage cheese consistency.

**Sudden jerks and twitches** – It's not her fault that her muscles seem to have a mind of their own. My husband and I used to quietly giggle by newborn Faith's bassinet as her arms would suddenly jet straight out in front of her then ever so slowly inch back down to her side. It was a routine at bedtime.

**Swollen and bloodshot eyes** are normal in the first few days. If after six weeks, it hasn't cleared up, check with your doctor.

**Tearless crying** – Ducts are maturing and this is nature's way of sparing parents those sad tears that would just be too much to bear in the beginning. Don't worry. In just a matter of weeks, full waterworks will be underway.

## Newborn FAQs

Q: "**My baby seems so fragile.** I'm afraid I'm going to break him as I change his clothes. His little head is so unstable. I don't know how to handle him. Can you help?"

A: **You do need to be careful about a baby's unstable neck** and never shake your baby for any reason. However, a baby is quite resilient and with a gentle and firm hand, he can be handled without worry for baths and changing. When holding or moving your baby, put your hand under his neck and the small of his back with the other hand under his buttocks and the top of his legs. Lift slowly and steadily and keep him close to your body and low to the ground when possible.

When putting on a shirt or onesie, stretch out the neck as far as possible and from the back of baby's head stretch up and over the head to the front. Then, put the arm opening over the baby's hand. Reach in the top of the opening and gently pull baby's hand out of the opening while pulling the rest of the clothing down over the arm and onto the torso. Next lift baby's body up by the legs and grab the shirt from behind and pull down to cover baby's body. Lastly, secure clothing together at the bottom. I suggest using drawstring or zippered clothing as much as possible in those first several weeks and avoid snaps and buttons.

Q: "Do you have any creative ideas on what to do with your child's newborn clothes that you won't need anymore?"

A: Save that one really special outfit in a shadow box. Give away others to someone about to give birth, do a clothing swap with other moms, or sell them at a second hand store. And, with all those clothes that are too cute to part with, try these suggestions:

1. Lay them all out on the floor and take a picture of the clothes. Then print out a photo and cut out the outline of the clothes. Then line them all up and paste them into a scrapbook. Above the clothes, draw a 'clothes line'. Voila! This is as cute as can be and takes up a lot less space then storing those clothes for years. Now, you can give away newborn baby clothes without really "giving them away completely."

2. Save the best of the best and let your children use them on their dolls. It will be a thrill for your child to 'share' in this way and you will keep the clothes close to your heart and home. Also, newborn diapers are much more economical than baby doll diapers.

Q: "**Diaper changes are so messy.** Do you have any tips on how to make it a less disastrous proposition?"

A: **Cloth diapers are handy and economical.** You can buy a dozen at a time and use them as burp cloths, lap protectors, and under baby during messy diaper changes. That way you can just remove the cloth diaper for cleaning instead of changing the entire changing table each time. Another option is to open up a fresh diaper and put it underneath the old diaper before you start changing. Also, before grabbing for a wipe, use the top of the dirty diaper to wipe "down and away" and get the majority of the mess. A tip for male babies is to quickly put a clean diaper over an exposed baby while cleaning or preparing for a fresh diaper. The last thing you need is waterworks to add to the mix.

If you find poops are not being contained, try moving up a size in diapers. Also, be sure to pull up the diaper in the back and secure straps so there are no gaps.

Q: "**I don't know where to start when giving my baby a bath.** Please help!"

A: **In the beginning, baths are more for stimulation** than cleaning so don't worry if you don't cover every crack and crevice. Concentrate on making it a soothing and pleasant experience for both you and baby. Use a damp washcloth (soap is optional) to wipe down baby. Start with the cleanest area (face) then progress to other areas, ending with the diaper area. When possible, keep baby's body covered when you are not cleaning it. For instance, when you are working on his hair, cover his entire body with a towel. Then, when you are doing the diaper area you can put a shirt on. If your baby seems cold, turn on the shower and steam up the bathroom for a few minutes before taking baby in for bath.

**Q:** **"I can't remember what the hospital said about umbilical cord and circumcision care.** Can you remind me?"

**A:** **Generously apply rubbing alcohol on a cotton ball and don't be shy about dousing the cord**. Even a squeeze of the cotton ball is okay. It's also safe to move the cord around a bit to be sure all areas are covered. Be sure to give time for the area to air dry. If you find moisture, puss, or redness, consult your doctor. The cord should fall off on its own within a couple of weeks.

Circumcised babies need a gentle touch, warm water for rinsing (3 times a day), petroleum jelly with each diaper change, and occasional use of antibiotic cream if your doctor has prescribed this. If there is a plastibell or a scab, either will fall off within 10 days.

# 3

# "Open W I D E ! ! !"

## Breast Milk, By Any Means Necessary

*Every third hour of the day, 2-week-old Faith would begin to get fussy and would escalate at an alarming rate if milk was not served within seconds. My husband would jokingly interpret the cries as "Can't you see I'm starving here? I haven't had a thing to eat all week! Feed me!" After feedings, Faith would be so calm and content and rest happily in welcoming arms. It was as if she had not known a sad moment in her life...well, that is, until that third hour rolled around again.*

Congratulations for choosing to give your baby breast milk. Did you know that if your baby was born prematurely that your breasts would produce just the type of milk suited to the age of your baby? And, even if you only gave your baby breast milk once a day, the benefits can still be measured. Since the most significant effects are measured in the first six months of breastfeeding, try to hang in there for at least that long. The benefits do not end with baby, either. Among other benefits, moms who nurse have a reduced chance of breast cancer and heal quicker after delivery. So, it's worth giving it your best shot for the sake of you and your baby.

**Although breastfeeding seems like it should be instinctual, it does not necessarily come naturally.** Both baby and mom need time to learn the technique as well as how to communicate with each other. Don't be alarmed if it takes up to 8 weeks to get really on track with this part of your journey. Most moms who say it didn't 'work' for them give up in the first couple of weeks. With the right information and support you can enjoy it as a very fulfilling part of motherhood. La Leche League is an invaluable resource for information, forums, as well as locating a lactation consultant when needed.

**Breast pumps come in handy for many reasons.** When you are engorged, pumping for a few minutes before nursing can make for easier latch-on. Also, if your baby has difficulty managing the flow that comes with letdown (this is when your milk really starts flowing and your baby starts sucking much faster), pumping for a few minutes before latch-on can help. Lastly, the best times to pump for the purpose of storage are first thing in the morning or one hour before a nursing session. Your milk production is lowest around dinnertime so refrain from pumping at that time.

**Sharing of breast pumps is considered unsafe.** Buy your own or rent through Medela.com. Although some moms are successful with hand expressing or using single pumps, my first choice is the Medela "Pump 'N Style" so you can efficiently pump both breasts at the same time. It's a financial investment, but worth it especially if there is the possibility of more children being added to your family.

**Once breastfeeding is successfully established, introduce the bottle when your baby is about three weeks old.** Once you start, give one bottle every day. Many moms stop after a couple of weeks thinking that baby has adjusted just fine, but then find that baby refuses the bottle at around 3 months when they try again. Even if you don't plan to return to work or be away from baby, it is still recommended to teach baby how to drink from a bottle, for you never know if baby will need expressed milk for a few days while you are battling an illness. Also, a bottle (middle of the night feeding) is a great way to have time for daddy to bond with baby as well as give mommy some shuteye.

**According to the La Leche League, you can store freshly expressed breast milk** without refrigeration for up to 4 hours and in the refrigerator for up to 8 days. It's normal for the milk to separate and need shaking. You can freeze breast milk for up to 3 months in the freezer or longer in a deep freezer, but some babies are particular about the change in taste. In that case, sell that liquid gold to a milk bank! To defrost, use warm water or defrost in refrigerator. Do not microwave or use hot water.

**Once the baby's mouth touches the bottle you cannot save the milk,** so I would suggest storing milk in portions of 2 to 3 ounces. If baby finishes the first 3 ounces, then put in another two ounces. The general rule of thumb is if baby drains the bottle, she would have taken more. Take baby's cues for how much is needed.

**Sometimes babies will want to add a feeding or nurse longer** during growth spurts (approximately at 3 wks, 6 wks, 9 wks,

**Enjoy the Ride**

3 months, 6 months, and 9 months) or you will want to drop a feeding to give a bottle. In both cases, the adjustment time is around 3-5 days to adjust to a new schedule. You may experience leakage in both cases. This is normal.

## Transition from Breast Milk to Formula

You might find the need to transition from breast milk to formula sometime before your baby is one-year-old. If this is the case, the best way to transition is to slowly add formula into breast milk feedings gradually until you end up having full formula feedings. Over the course of a few days you should be able to determine if there are any allergies and make adjustments as necessary. Whenever you introduce anything new to your baby, watch closely for allergic reactions for at least 24 hours afterwards. Reactions come in the form of rash, itch, fussiness, or difficulty breathing. It is normal for poop to change in consistency (firmer) and color (grey, brown, green), but white or black tarry (tar-like) poop warrants a call to your doctor. In all cases, consult your doctor if you have suspicion of an allergic reaction, but in the latter case, seek medical attention immediately.

16

## Nursing Schedule for Working Mom

If you'd like to continue with breastfeeding while offering formula at some feedings, it is very possible to sustain milk to feed first thing in the morning and last thing before bed. Many moms find this to be a very satisfying schedule for the 10-12 months old and up, especially if Mom is working outside the home during the day. Many moms can continue nursing for several months on this schedule.

*Why is she crying? Every time I start nursing, she latches on for a couple seconds and then falls off and cries as if she's really mad! As both of us are shedding too many tears for comfort, I resort to giving my baby a bottle of glucose water because I am so afraid that she is starving. What I didn't know was that the few drops of colostrum she was getting from me was infinitely better for her than glucose water, and what's more, giving her a bottle was jeopardizing my efforts to successfully breastfeed.*

## Keeping Track of Diapers

In those early days, it's important to keep track of the number of wet and dirty diapers and to consult your doctor if you are concerned that your baby is not getting enough fluids. In the first few days, expect just 1-3 wet and 1-3 dirty diapers a day. Bowel movements will be sticky and dark, progressing to yellowish by the third or fourth day. By this time, your baby should have about 3-4 wet diapers and 3-4 poopy diapers a day. By day 5-6, your baby should be having 3-5 loose stools per day and 4-5 very wet diapers a day. Up until week 8, you should see about 4-6 wet diapers and 2-3 bowel movements a day. Remember that these are just averages and that if your baby seems to be eating well and is happy and alert, that is a good indicator of how they are doing overall. However, if at any time you are concerned or uneasy about how your baby seems to be doing, always check with your health professional for evaluation and assurance. (See appendix for feeding chart and helpful schedules)

## Nipple Confusion

If you're one of the lucky few, then your baby will have no preference over breast or bottle and you will be able to easily switch back and forth. However, if you are amongst those whose baby has taken a preference to the bottle because of early introduction (before breastfeeding has been successfully established), then be prepared for some work ahead.

Be encouraged. Although there might be tears from both mom and baby during this learning process, rest assured that if you are committed, then there is a great chance for success. Unless your baby has a physical condition (which can be corrected in consultation with your doctor) that interferes with the ability to nurse, if you remain steadfast, breastfeeding can still be successfully established even after baby has been on a bottle exclusively for weeks. Even moms who change their minds and want to re-start breastfeeding after baby is 8 weeks old can have success if they are committed to make it work.

Here is the process. Once you decide that you're "all in", set aside the next 72 hours to give it your best shot and then go for it. It will be tempting to resort to giving a bottle especially when it seems that baby is not getting enough from the breast, but try to think long-term. These few short days of struggle will seem like nothing once you have a happy baby at breast. If you still want to supplement for ease of mind, try using a spoon or syringe to hydrate baby, but stay away from the bottle or you will be back to square one.

Look for a big, open mouth that looks like a yawn and pull her in close. Although there might be an uncomfortable sensation at first or during letdown, excruciating pain is a cue that she is not latched on correctly. Your goal is to get baby on breast as many times as possible to have satisfying feeding sessions, which usually means at least 20 minutes total feeding time. Take baby's cues to see when she's had enough. One trick that I would use as a last resort is to drip expressed milk or glucose water onto breast while trying to get baby to latch on. She will taste the milk and start sucking more vigorously which will give you time to get her correctly latched on. Be patient and remember that you are both learning.

# 4

# "Rock-a-Bye Baby"

## Sleep for Baby/Toddler

*What would happen if you got up at 3 a.m. and had a BLT and a glass of milk? How long do you think it would take for you to begin to automatically wake up hungry at that same time every night? When I was a teacher, I always needed to use the restroom at 10:15 a.m. and was hungry for lunch at 11:30 a.m. Even on vacation, my system was so conditioned to this schedule that it was hard to ignore those regulated pangs of hunger.*

**Babies as young as a few days old can begin to develop these rhythms for sleep and feedings.** I know there are some who don't believe in schedules for babies, but I believe that routine feedings aid in developing regular sleep habits and makes for a happy baby.

**Insure your baby gets a full, satisfying feeding each time at breast or bottle.** I believe that for most babies it will be fairly easy to adjust to feeding around every 2½ to 3 hours throughout the day. Please don't withhold food when there is a growth spurt or a true need for nutrition, (Please check with doctor if you have any question that your baby is not getting enough food, as there could be physical reasons for it), but overall if you work toward this routine, I believe that you and baby will be very satisfied. Your baby will be able to settle into a nap long enough to progress through all the necessary stages of sleep while giving you enough time to catch a breath, pay a bill, or take a nap yourself.

## Tips

**It's normal for babies to wake mid-nap and several times during the night, but they do not need to feed every time they wake.** Sometimes they need 10-15 minutes to resettle and progress into a deep sleep. Sometimes they need to pass gas or have a hearty old-fashioned belch. Try to distinguish between the different types of cries so that you can meet their needs more effectively. Don't assume that every cry means they are hungry.

**Consider sleeping in a different room than your newborn.** Getting a good quality video monitor (digital ones have the least amount of interference) will allow you to see your baby even at night. This added sense of security can aid in your ability to get some rest and to allow you and your baby to not be disturbed by the others' natural sounds and movements during the night. Because the sound part of the monitor is extra sensitive and will make even the smallest stir sound much more serious, turn the volume off, low, or turn it on once in a while to check in. Let the sight of safe baby be enough for you. Even without a monitor, you'll be able to hear when a visit from Mom or Dad is necessary.

**Set a predictable routine and be consistent.** Babies love routine even at the beginning. Consider daily walks around the same time of day. Play the same song at each bath. Try a bedtime routine with something soothing like: bath time, song/story time, milk, and then bed. When your schedule requires flexibility in this routine, allow for it, but do your best to get back on this comforting routine as much as possible.

**Wean from sleep props before the third month of life.** No pacifiers, bottles, or rocking. Habits that go beyond this time frame are very difficult to break. Teach baby to soothe himself to sleep and stay asleep.

**Consider the use of white noise** in the form of fan, radio, or sound machine (wave, rain, etc.) especially when you have siblings' sleep to consider. This is also handy during sleep training sessions for infants as it tempers the sound of the crying but does not block out parents' awareness of what is going on. Remember that monitors magnify sound. It's rarely as bad as it sounds. When they really need you, you will hear it-monitor or not.

**When transitioning from bassinet to crib,** many babies are comforted when you move the bassinet mattress into the crib and/or make their sleeping area in the crib smaller. Try to bring familiar smells and feels into the new sleep area, but remain conscious of toys, pillows, and blankets that baby could possibly roll into or move too close to. These items have been associated with SIDS (sudden infant death syndrome) and should be avoided in the first three months of life.

**When moving from crib to bed around 2-3 years,** start with daytime naps, progressing to nighttime. Sometimes with a new sib-ling's eminent arrival, you need to start early, but I suggest keeping your child in the crib as long as possible and is safe. If there are attempts at climbing, make the change immediate. At first, try the bed mattress on the floor or with a bed rail. I find a video monitor very handy for this time of transition. As all parents can attest to, sometimes "too quiet" means something is up, so it's nice to have a view of the room at all times.

**For older children, set guidelines for quiet in the morning** until all members of the household are awake. Agree on a household 'Start of the Day' time and out of respect for all members of the family, require quiet activity until that time.

*One day, 4-year-old Hope came into my room after waiting for what seemed like an eternity to her. "Mommy, can it be morning, now, please?" "Yes, honey, I declare it morning...Tada!"*

# 5

# "Stay by My Cradle?"

## Sleep for Everyone

*I distinctly remember sitting with 4 year- old Grace one day and enjoying the song "Are You Sleeping?" We were singing it in rounds over and over again. After the last verse, I turned to see Grace sitting quietly and pondering with that far off look that meant she was about to ask a thought-provoking question. She turned to me and asked, "Mommy? Who is the little sister of brother John?"*

In my parenting consulting business, the concern of having children sleep through the night is the number one issue by far. In talking with so many parents over this issue, I realize that it is in fact emotionally harder on the parent than the child. Many parents are concerned that teaching their child to sleep when they don't want to do so might somehow cause them emotional damage, but let me demonstrate how this is not true.

When 3-year-old Faith was going through a season of getting out of her bed at night, we were allowing her time to settle and not responding to whiny requests. After a few minutes of quiet, she started calling out in a high-pitched voice, "Mommy, Daddy??" over and over. Although it was hard not to respond, with a quick peek at the video monitor, we were certain that she was just testing to see if we'd come in. A moment later she confirmed our suspicions with these quiet and composed words to herself: "Why Mommy, Daddy is not coming?? Maybe if I cry. Wahhh...wahhh...wahhh...Mommy, Daddy?" She waited a few moments in silence to see if we would come to the rescue and then resigned to falling asleep a few minutes later.

Don't wait for your child's approval to teach them to get enough rest. You are the parent and know what's best. It's okay that you guide your child into healthy sleeping habits. His complaining is meant to sway you and tug at you emotionally, but if you stand strong (usually just 3-5 days), the long-term benefits of healthy sleep for everyone in the family will be well worth it. You will wish you had started earlier.

Q: "I try to keep my baby up for most of the day so that he will be tired and sleep through the night. Is that the best way?"

A: A well-rested baby sleeps peacefully at night. Some people assume that babies who sleep too much during the day will be up at night, but the opposite is true. Rhythms of play and a few naps a day lasting 1 ½ to 2 hours will keep baby from becoming over-stimulated during the day and ready for a good night's sleep.

Q: "When can I expect my baby to sleep through the night?"

A: In my experience, it is 2-3 months of age or around the time babies reach 13 pounds that they seem ready to go without food for 8-12 hours at a time. A baby may wake at 3 a.m. every night out of habit, but usually by this time they are ready to stretch out their feedings.

Q: "My 3-month-old is crying at night and waking my 5-year-old up from sleep. I get her quickly so that she doesn't cry for long, but it's becoming a routine. Can you help?"

A: Try to think long-term. It's understandable to be concerned about everyone's sleep at night, but once your baby gets the hang of falling asleep on his own, your entire household will enjoy night after night of uninterrupted slumber. In the meantime, create some white noise for your older child so his sleep has less chance of being disturbed.

Q: "What's a normal amount of time for an average 1-year-old to sleep in a day?"

A: Every baby is an individual and will sleep different amounts of time when compared to other babies. However, in my experience, there is a reliable range of average sleep, give or take an hour or two.

Newborns average around 17-18 hours a day, only waking for feedings and very short periods of wakefulness.

As babies grow over the first year, they gradually sleep less in a 24-hour period, but a one-year-old can still sleep an aver-age of 15-16 hours a day. For babies who are guided during the day and night as I've described in previous chapters, night time sleep ranges from 10-12 hours with two naps that are 1 ½ to 2 hours long each during the day.

Typically around 15 months to 2 years, children move to one 2-3 hour nap shortly after lunch.

Around the fourth or fifth birthday, children continue with only the 10-12 hours of sleep at night.

After that, the transition to less sleep is very slow and gradual with a ten-year-old sleeping about 8-10 hours at night.

# 6

# "Here Comes the Choo-Choo"

## How, When, and What to Feed Your Child

*Recipe for a Picky Eater*

*3 snacks before each mealtime, including juice*
*1 tbsp of sugar added to every meal*
*1 ounce of permission to eat only what they like*
*1 promise of dessert as a bribe for eating their veggies*

*Mix all ingredients together thoroughly and bake for 20 minutes each day, three times a day. Coax for 10 minutes, and then serve. Enjoy!*

According to the American Academy of Pediatrics, you need not rush your child to start solids because he is getting his needs met from breast milk or formula for the first four to six months of life. Also, there is more of a chance for allergic reactions to foods if introduced before that time. When ready, and in consultation with your pediatrician, you can begin the process of introducing solids little by little.

**Around four to six months of age, you might notice your child is hungry more often, is intently watching you eat, or actually reaching out for your food. In this case, he might be ready to start on rice cereal.** Pediatricians recommend to start with rice cereal mixed with breast milk or formula and to feed with a spoon, not in a bottle. After 3-5 days (watch for signs of allergy like rash, runny nose, or difficulty breathing), progress to oatmeal, barley cereal, then mixed cereal. Gradually make the mixture thicker as baby learns to move food from the front of his mouth to the back. In the next couple months, he should be having 4-5 feedings of breast milk or formula and four or more tablespoons of food a day.

**Once the cereals are established (around 6-7 months), I like to recommend offering the blandest foods first** so that a preference for sweeter foods is not developed early on. I have known many babies who start with bananas and other fruit and thereby become particular about greens and meats later on. Start with all the green, then orange veggies, and then the fruits. Offer one new food at a time for 5 days before moving to the next in order to check for allergies. Once a food has been successfully tested, you can start to combine, as you need. Don't worry about offering veggies during a time that an adult would normally consider to be breakfast. Babies are not particular about that. At this time, it is a good time to introduce a few ounces of 100% fruit juice. Start with pear, peach, and white grape, but avoid apple juice, as it tends to be less nutritious. Start with a sippy cup, but be firm about weaning from bottle around one year and from sippy cup shortly after your child shows mastery of drinking from a regular cup. If you wait much after this, it can be more difficult to give up but also there has been evidence that extended use of sippy cups can contribute towards delays in dental development as well as speech development.

**Doctors recommend that around 8-9 months you can begin to introduce meat, cheese, egg yolks (not whites), and yogurt.** Avoid whole milk, nuts, grapes, raw honey, citrus, and tomato-based products, as well. Some doctors allow peanut butter at this time, but check with your pediatrician for specific recommendations. (See feeding chart in the appendix) You can also start to add finger foods at this point. Try soft, cubed veggies and fruits, pastas, string cheese, tofu, seaweed, soybeans, rice, crackers, and of course Cheerios and Goldfish. At the rate my children went through these, I should have bought stock in Goldfish crackers years ago!

**By age one, your child will be joining the rest of the family for meals.** They should be eating three times a day at the same times as the family. They should be able to eat just about everything else your family is eating for dinner, but in smaller portions and pieces. Help to make them feel a part of the family by including them in conversation.

**One trick I've used when cooking for the whole family is to initially cook all meats and veggies with no seasoning.** When the food is all cooked, then I'd take out a portion for my child. Afterwards I'd add special seasonings, seafood, or nuts to the food and serve to the others in the family. This served a couple purposes. On the one hand, it prevented the need to cook two separate meals multiple times a day. On the other, the youngest members of the family quickly grew accustomed to the family's menu and it was a good way to ease them into the family routine.

**Persuasion. It's good for so many things, but let's leave it out of the equation when at the dinner table.** Besides, when was the last time you had to say to your husband, "Okay, now honey, open wide for the airplane?" Let's focus on making mealtimes a peaceful and enjoyable time for all. It may take some time to get to this point, but be patient in the process, and it will pay off. One day, not only will home meals around the table be enjoyable, but you will also be welcome guests wherever you go.

Here are some tips on making mealtimes pleasant for everyone around the table. Remember that the goal of mealtime is not only to have a meal but for all those around the table to enjoy the entire process, as well.

**Limit snacks and liquids** so that your children will have had nothing 2 hours before a mealtime. Trying to make children sit still, eat, and enjoy the time when they are not hungry is like trying to make them sleep after a three hour nap.

**Set an example** and come to the table with a positive attitude, ready to share, listen, and enjoy a meal together. Wait until everyone is seated before beginning to eat and stay seated until everyone is finished eating.

**Reinforce positive behavior** by making remarks like, "Wow, you just gobbled up all that broccoli; I think I see your muscles growing!" or "You are sitting so quietly and patiently." or "Thank you for waiting for me to sit at the table."

**Make your expectations clear.** If you don't expect much, you won't get much. Reiterate your expectations, post them, and model what you want to see. (Consult chapter 20 for an explanation of our family's table manners poster.)

**Teach to take turns over sharing.** Most toddlers learn to say "no" and "mine" without any specific coaching or teaching on the subject. Although ownership is a positive concept and children should be allowed to embrace ownership of their belongings at times, it is important to teach your little ones the joy of sharing. Many times the term "share" is harder to accept than "taking turns" so present plenty of opportunities to model what you expect and give plenty of chances to practice, fail, and enjoy success. Using timers or counting while expressing satisfaction and joy in watching others enjoy their turn can be a great experience for all.

**Use humor.** Age 5 and up: Ask everyone to share something funny that happened that day. Try the game, "Two Truths and a Lie" where everyone shares two things that really happened that day and one that didn't. Everyone guesses which is not true. Be careful not to choke on your food because this game produces guaranteed laughter at the table. For the younger members of the family, help them to distinguish between fantasy and reality as sometimes the content of their sharing can be affected by their desire to get a reaction from family members.

*When Grace was 3 years old, just for fun, my husband would use reverse psychology and say things like "Now, honey, you're not going to eat up ALL those veggies, riiiiigghht? You don't want to grow such big muscles or you...OH, no! Stop! You're eating too many!" Hee, hee...*

*We never realized that this was something that Grace really thought about and enjoyed. One day, while quietly eating, she picked up a forkful of peas and said, "Okay, daddy, joke it up!" At first we didn't understand what she meant, but then realized she had enjoyed those comments so much and that it made eating really fun for her.*

**Offer a variety of foods** in a colorful array. Talk to your children about the value of having a varied diet. You need to set a good example. Of course you have to sneak in the occasional chocolate when they are not looking, but be careful.

**A word regarding introducing your child to a cup.** If your child doesn't seem to take to the myriad of options of sippy cups that you've introduced him to, consider going straight to a soft rimmed cup, one with a straw, or one with an open spout and no insert that slows down the flow. Some babies even take to water served from a spoon. Whatever brings success, be persistent and re-introduce and re-try until your little one is enjoying beverages like a big kid!

*One day when I tried to inconspicuously pop a miniscule piece of chocolate into my mouth, I heard 3-year-old Faith saying, "I smmmmmelllll chocolate!!" Even to this day, she has a sixth sense that signals when chocolate is within a 10-mile radius.*

## Tips on Feeding the Toddler

"My baby has always been a great eater until he turned 18 months. Then, everything changed! Fussy eating and food battles began!"

Around the time from 18 months to 3 years, your child's growth slows down dramatically. Also, they are becoming much more independent and struggling both with wanting to be close and wanting to be separate from parents. Don't be alarmed if your child eats much less than usual.

Offer a variety of foods on a regular and consistent basis and avoid food battles. At the end of a mealtime, clear food and try again at the next meal. Give small and healthful snacks in between meals, but be sure to not offer snacks too close to mealtime.

To help ease the toddler parent's mind, here are some tips and information about a toddler and their eating habits.

1. For a child one or two years old, the rate of growth is only half to a third that of the infant up to age 12 months.

2. It's normal for toddler appetites to be erratic and sporadic.

3. Toddlers want more to be independent than to eat. If you participate in food battles, you will face more challenges in the food arena.

4. Children at this age grow in height more quickly than gain weight and they lose body fat, using stored fat for part of energy needs.

5. Look to your child for cues on nourishment. If they are active and alert and overall happy, then they are most likely well-nourished. A poorly nourished child would sit in the corner and be lethargic and reclusive.

6. Once your toddler is efficient with utensil usage, provide closely supervised opportunities to use at mealtime. Remember to use limit-setting in learning proper usage of utensils and appropriate manners at the table.

What does my child really need?

You'd be surprised and reassured that a toddler actually does not as much in a day as you might think.

Every meal should include:
-a protein (meat, fish, poultry, egg, cooked dried beans, seeds or nuts),
-bread or cereal (bread, bun, noodles)
-fruit or vegetable or both
-and milk.

Here are some ideas on portions:

1. Toddlers need about 2-3 cups of milk per day. If they have more than that, you risk your child being too full to get in the other nutrients needed during the day. Water should be offered for thirst.

2. Your child needs four servings of fruits and vegetables per day. An adequate portion size is one tablespoon per year of age.

3. Offer enriched or whole grain breads and cereals. A child's serving is about ¼ of an adult sized portion. The adult serving would be one slice of bread, five crackers, or 1/2cup rice or pasta. Many children prefer this food group over the others and there is nothing wrong with that as long as the minimum requirement from the other groups is also met.

4. About 2 servings (1oz) of protein is sufficient for toddlers. Try beans, beef, chicken, tuna, soybeans, or tofu. If your child has difficulty chewing meat, try to mix it into casseroles,

soups, patties, etc. Avoid processed meats like hotdogs as there is a large amount of salt.

When evaluating your child's diet, consider the big picture. Calculate the average intake over a week. If your child eats more of one thing one day, don't worry. It will balance out over the course of a week if you offer a variety at each meal. Ideally, each food group should be offered each day.

Make mealtime fun. It's a time to sit and enjoy your food in the company of those you love. Make it a memorable experience for all.

# 7

# "Me Do It"

## Speech Development

One day, 3-year-old Grace decided she wanted to tuck ME in to bed. She carefully pulled the covers away and waited for me to get in. Then, she covered me and knelt at my bedside to pray. The bed was so high I couldn't even see her head when I looked over, but then I heard these precious words that touched my heart. "Dear God, help her do good dreams and bless her good at night and don't let her get scared and give sweet dreams. Amen."

We are working to model and teach accurate speech, but there is something to be said about the beauty in the way a 3-year-old speaks. Take time to notice, savor, and record these moments along the way. As your child grows you'll want to help him develop strong verbal skills. Here are some tips that will help you get off to a good start.

   Although it's very tempting, avoid the urge to use "baby talk." Instead, as much as you can, model correct pronunciation and grammar. Aim vocabulary a little higher than you think is understood. Of course you want to be understood, but you also want to stretch little minds so children can make connections and inferences, and use context for meaning. For instance, if he says, "Down chair" you can respond by saying, "Oh, do you want to get down from your highchair?" He may only understand a few of the words you use, but with repetition and making connections over time, he will not only understand what a 'highchair' is, but he will begin to add that vocabulary word to the little dictionary being built in his minds.

   The single best thing you can do to help your child with not only speech development, but also vocabulary, comprehension, and reading readiness, is to read aloud to your child daily. In the *Read Aloud Handbook* by Jim Trelease he says that "listening comprehension must come before reading comprehension" and that

"regular reading aloud strengthens children's reading, writing, and speaking skills– and thus the entire civilizing process." Start this activity as early as when your child is three weeks old, at which time he is becoming more responsive to his surroundings. Read books a bit above what you think he completely understand and model reading with enthusiasm. Choose books with colorful pictures, familiar objects or experiences and talk about them in a way that sparks interest. It's hard for a child not to love reading when a parent models passion for it. As Jim Trelease says, "Reading aloud is the best advertisement because it works. It allows a child to sample the delights of reading and conditions him to believe that reading is a pleasureful experience, not a painful or boring one."

**As your children get older, spend time having them read to you, too.** However, be careful not to have that substitute the time you spend enjoying a fascinating novel with them. Discussing the plot and interesting moments in the story and relating it to their own personal experience will build wonderful and bonding memories together.

### Using Sign Language

Around the age when babies can clap and wave (7-9 months), expose your child to sign language. Although some people believe that the use of sign language stunts speech development, the opposite is actually true. With this building block to language, she will learn to speak earlier and more proficiently. Studies show that children who use sign language have higher IQ's. Sign language also eases typical toddler frustration in not being able to express themselves before much verbal language is possible, thus reducing the number of frustration tantrums.

## "Da Da Da Da...Ma!"

Much to the disappointment of mothers everywhere, babies often say "Da Da" before they learn to say "Ma Ma." It has been said that this is not only true in English but other languages as well. A few thoughts here. First of all, psychologists have said that babies see themselves as one with their moms so they don't distinguish between themselves and mom. They, however, hear much talk about 'daddy', a separate entity. Secondly, it has been hypothesized that perhaps the reason babies often say "Da Da" first, is that there is an inherent desire in babies to bond with their daddies. There's something about that father-child relationship that is crucial in the development of a child. So, whatever your child says, whether they're saying, "Da Da" to an uncle or "Ma Ma" to their dolly, enjoy this new development and know that they do, indeed, love you both!

# 8

# "Make a Wish"

## Celebrations

*When 2-year-old Faith woke up on the morning of her birthday, I came in and said, "Do you know what a special day today is?" Her reply was, "It's Happy to You, Faith-y!"*

Who doesn't love a birthday party? Here are some suggestions for celebrating birthdays in meaningful, yet simple ways.

**Avoid the temptation to throw a big party for your child *just because*** it is expected and because you feel the need to reciprocate invitations to other parties. Instead, consider what would be meaningful for your child. It could be that a family outing to a local park or purchasing that one special item that she's had her eye on all year is enough for her.

**Consider combining the celebrations** if you have two or more children with birthdays within two months of each other. One party works really well if you would have invited most of the same guests anyway. Not only can this save you time, energy, and money, but it also makes it easier on your guests' schedules.

**How much sleep do they really get at sleepovers?** Consider a mock sleep over that starts at 5 p.m. (with dinner) and ends at 9 p.m. Kids enjoy all the fun of a sleep over (PJs, food, a video and chats) and parents picking up children ready for bed and a good night's rest. This is great for kids who are either too young for sleepovers, or have parents who are reluctant to leave their children at your house overnight.

**In honor of your child's birthday, consider throwing a party for another child** who has a birthday the same month and who is less apt to have a birthday party thrown in his/her honor. Or, in lieu of gifts, have guests bring in-kind donations for a selected charity. The birthday gift your child receives that year is compassion and generosity.

**Encourage simple, but meaningful gift giving between siblings.** Instead of perusing the toy store aisles for something to buy for a sibling's birthday, encourage your children to make gifts and cards and be creative. One year, 7-year-old Grace decorated a cute plastic frame and wrote an acrostic with her sister's name. Years later it still adorns Faith's room.

**Reflect on the past year with your child.** Think of the successes and growth as well as the challenges she has overcome or that she is still working through. Consider writing an annual birthday letter to your child to express how proud you are of her, and how much you look forward to the new year ahead.

**Create simple annual traditions** that everyone will look forward to year after year. For example, purchase or make a birthday plate to serve cake or a special meal. It's a simple idea that will make the birthday person feel honored. Encourage others in the family to prepare the plate and serve the guest of honor.

**Who says candles only go on cakes?** Improvise and create surprises as you adorn a breakfast pancake, a piece of jello, or a dinner roll with a candle and song. Remember, it's always the thought that counts!

## Daddy and Mommy Dates

*My husband's tradition was to take each of our daughters on a "Daddy Date" for their birthday, I decided that I wanted in on the fun too and started the "Mommy Date" for their half birthday. As with the daddy date, the birthday girl gets to choose the restaurant to have their special celebration. It is hard for Hope to think beyond the restaurant with the golden arches, so we've been known to pick up food for a picnic and play at a nearby park. The older kids have enjoyed places where birthdays are recognized with balloons hanging from their ears or by walking around with pixie dust to sprinkle restaurant guests with birthday joy. After each outing, the unbirthday siblings and dad have half a cake and half a birthday song waiting at home "Happy birthday dear Fai~" stop and giggle. The best part of both Mommy and Daddy dates is that each parent gets uninterrupted time with each child, and that is a gift on which you cannot put a price tag.*

*When Grace was 6 years old, she told her friends at school about how she celebrated her half birthday and their response was, "Aw, you're so lucky, I don't have a half birthday!" She'd reply, "Yes, you do too!!" and then she would immediately begin calculating for them the date of their half birthdays. This helped to make many of her friends feel special as they began to be recognized for this milestone in their lives as well.*

## Christmas Holidays

Once the holiday season rolls around, it's time to get ready to prepare for the biggest birthday party of them all: Jesus' birthday!

Here are some tips to keep the season simple and fun, yet meaningful.

1. Bake a cake and sing "Happy Birthday" to Jesus
2. Wrap gifts and put them under the tree for Jesus. Consider creative expressions of gifts like birthday cards, promises written on pretty cards, acts of service (then wrap a picture of you having done the service), write a list of people you will pray for that year, etc.
3. Make invitations and invite people to come celebrate the most important birthday of all.
4. Reflect as a family and individually what Jesus has meant in your life over the past year.
5. Sing worship songs or hymns as you sit by the CHRISTmas tree.
6. Do a service project together as a family like serving food in a soup kitchen, delivering toys and clothing to an orphanage, serving an elderly neighbor by doing chores around the house for them, etc.

7. Bring back the art of caroling to your neighborhood. Your kids will love this and so will the neighbors.

8. Bake cookies and share with your neighbors, especially those whom you do not know.

9. Begin Christmas morning with individual quiet times and then gather together to pray before you share gifts.

10. Make the holiday more about the people than the presents!

# PART TWO

—

## Two To Five Years

# 9

# "I Be Dry, Mama!"
## Potty Training

*One evening at the dinner table, Faith started to share a joke and then stopped to say that it was not appropriate to tell at that time. Grace leaned over and in a voice that she thought only Faith could hear said, "Is it about poo-poo?"*

I was standing in front of my daughter's classroom and over-heard some parents discussing their apprehension over starting potty training with a two-year-old. One parent found comfort in sending their child to daycare to be trained so that the responsibility did not rest with the parents. Time after time, I've heard parents dreading this part of the parenting journey when it's just a simple route that all must take.

Here's my advice: Keep it simple. Don't lose sleep over a normal developmental milestone that your child will eventually reach. If you are anxious, your child will be stressed about the whole proposition. If you are matter-of-fact about it and understand that with trial and error your child will eventually learn, then the whole process will be much smoother for all involved.

## Potty Training Tips

**When you see readiness signs** (dry after nap and for two hours at a time during the day; noticing/announcing when they are wet and dry; at least 15 mo old) seize the opportunity and begin training.

**Without any fanfare,** talk to them about the transition they will need to make. They used to use the diaper, but now it's time to use the toilet.

**Don't go back to diapers** once you start training. It sends mixed signals about expectations and commitment.

**Double sheet the beds with sheets and sheet protectors** so that if there is an accident in the middle of the night it will allow for quick removal of wet sheets with a set of dry sheets underneath. Laundry can wait until morning.

**If you need to be out in public during the time of learning** and you don't want to leave the library with a special 'gift' in the form of a puddle then consider having your child wear underwear then pull-ups over them. That way they can still feel if they're wet, but the public does not need to 'feel' it.

**Avoid stickers, treats, and parties** when your child has success and on the flip side, avoid criticism and extreme disappointment at failures. Both bring too much pressure to the process. Instead, give verbal encouragement, but let him feel that the success is more about him than about Mom and Dad.

**Speed Toilet-Training** is possible if your child is at least 2 ½ years old and shows all the readiness signs. Consult *Toilet Training in Less Than a Day* by Nathan Azrin to read about how to use a doll to train your toddler.

**Talk about your habits.** It sounds funny, but it's helpful to talk about your toileting habits with your child so that he understands the whole process and knows that it's a normal thing that all people (and even animals) do. Say things like, "Oh, I drank that water and now I feel full and like I need to go to the potty." Then have him come with you and watch. Talk about the feeling of 'holding' and 'releasing.' Talk about how glad you are that you stayed dry and that being grown-up means always using the potty. This is a good time to demonstrate good habits, like closing the lid before flushing and washing your hands thoroughly afterwards.

**Put away all diapers.** Tell your child that there will be no more diapers in the house and go shopping with her to buy underwear. Explain that this is what she will be wearing from now on, day and night, and that the goal is to keep them dry.

**Plan regular times to visit the restroom.** I like to use the potty seats that go directly on the toilet, but if your child is big enough, go without. Plan to have your child sit on the toilet first thing in the morning, before and after each nap, after every meal, and before bedtime. Many parents also have success with the time just before a bath when running water serves as a cue. Also, when you notice he is dry after a couple hours, then that is a great time to sit on the toilet. Let him know he can go anytime as needed in addition, but it helps to regulate by having regular sessions in the beginning.

**Avoid fanfare of musical chairs, talking seats, and** other fancy equipment. It's not recommended to use any type of object to lure or motivate your child to use the toilet. The only motivation to learn should be learning itself. Of course, a celebration of new underwear shopping once your child has been dry for a full week is something that is reinforcing and fun for all. Just make sure you are reinforcing the idea that it is your child's accomplishment and focus more on his pride than yours.

**During the training period, think elastic.** Make it as easy as possible for your child to pull down his pants as quickly as possible without having to think about snaps, buttons, or hooks. You want all things working for and not against them so favor elastic pants and avoid complicated layers while in the training process.

**Consider the use of portable potties** when traveling on long car trips. Stash one in the back of the car to pull out in cases where a clean restroom in nowhere in sight. Using a plastic bag to line the seat can aide in easy cleanup.

**Be matter-of-fact about accidents.** It's a normal part of the process so don't make a big production out of it. Just say, "Oops, pee goes in the potty!" and then walk him to the potty and show and reiterate that this is where he needs to go. Then, proceed to help him clean up, and move on...

Remember, learning to use the toilet is a normal developmental skill and your child will learn how to be successful. Competence will come and much of how that happens will be determined by your approach and attitude. Give your child time and practice and enjoy even this part of the adventure.

*After sitting on the potty for some time while reading books and doing some serious business, we hear, "Phew! Glad that's over. The chubbies on my bottom were getting sweaty!"*

# 10

# "There's a Monster Under My Bed"

## Handling Night Terrors & Nightmares

*"I don't know what to do because every night I have bad, bad dreams, and all the yesternights are the same..." –Three-year-old Hope*

A couple hours after your 10-month-old child has fallen asleep, loud screaming and banging noises awaken you and you rush into his room to find him thrashing around in his fitful, sweaty sleep. His eyes are open and he looks alarmed and confused. You reach out to hold him and he fights you, pushing you away while crying harder. In a matter of minutes, he settles down and falls back asleep. You wonder if he had a bad dream or if something else is bothering him.

**The description above is typical of a night terror, which is often confused for a nightmare.** Although you may feel the need to intervene during an episode, it is neither necessary nor advisable. Although a child's eyes are open, he is actually still asleep and he will most likely not remember what happened the following morning. It's frightening and worrisome for parents to witness a night terror, but rest assured, the only thing you need to do is make sure the areas around your child are safe so that he doesn't bump into anything during the episode. It will pass quickly and will probably not happen on a regular basis. Night terrors can begin as early as when children are six months old and continue into the elementary school years. Night terrors can be hereditary. Be aware that stress or over tiredness can bring them on. If they happen more frequently than a few times a year, then consult your doctor, as it could be related to a medical condition. For more detailed information on night terrors, consult *www.nightterrors.org*, a comprehensive website resource on the topic.

**Nightmares, on the other hand, most typically occur after a 3- or 4-year-old child has been asleep for several hours** when he is in the REM (rapid eye movement) stage of sleep. He actually awaken s after the nightmare and still feels fearful. After a nightmare, children will want to cling to you and be consoled. Although nightmare episodes are brief, it will take varying amounts of time, depending on the child, to feel settled enough to go back to sleep.

Around age 3, vivid imaginations contribute to more active dreaming and sometimes frequent nightmares. Here is a glimpse of how we have handled it in our home.

As a general rule we avoid any movie, TV show, book, or even a song that might elicit feelings of fear in our children. Even if it's a fleeting image on a movie trailer, we do our best to protect their little minds from visual or audio experiences that could stay with them through the day and entertain their thoughts into the night. To counteract negative images they inevitably are exposed to, we also surround them with children's books that empower them to battle bad dreams. For example, one of our favorites describes a green monster in a way that gives children authority over it. *Go Away Big Green Monster* by Ed Emberley is a great resource to have on hand. Another is *Be Brave, Anna* by JoDee McConnaughhay which describes a dad giving his daughter tools to get through a night feeling safe and secure.

During the day and at bedtime, we suggest visual pictures of protection during the night that can help ease the process of lying alone in the dark while falling asleep and anticipating a nightmare. We give them the soothing image of beautiful and strong angels posted at each corner of their bed warding off all the 'bad dreams'. As they are about to drift off to hopefully sweet dreams, we sing them soothing songs and talk to them about funny or happy memories so that is the last thing on their minds before sleep.

We assure our children that all dreams are imaginary and that they can have some power in either ending their dream or changing its course. We suggest trying to tickle the monster or make jokes in their dreams. In talking about the dream and images, sometimes they can find some humor in the situation as they realize there is no such thing as a 20-foot Teletubby (Okay, that would scare me too...).

*"You know what I do when there are monsters in my dream? I make friends with them, and then we go off and play!!" –Six-year-old Grace*

# 11

# "Because I Said So!"

## Setting Limits

*I will never forget that moment when my sweet 18-month-old Faith, who could do no wrong, looked at me straight in the eye when I told her not to touch an outlet strip, and then continued to reach her hand closer and closer with that little gleam in her eye. It was a moment of truth.*

You're hesitant to take your child out to a restaurant or you have to sprint through the grocery store because you don't know what might happen if you linger. Does this sound familiar? When you start to notice your child directly challenging your authority, it's time to begin to set some limits. This can happen as early as six months old or may not happen until close to a child's second birthday.

Many parents believe what makes their children happiest is to give them freedom and pretty much whatever their little hearts desire. They think that playing with food is a creative expression or that taking away something a child wants is somehow damaging their self-esteem. There is insecurity in too much freedom. Or sometimes parents don't set limits because they don't expect that they can be accepted. Your children know when you feel this way so you have already lost the battle even before you begin. Remember that your children are far more capable to accept limits than you anticipate, and that limits actually make them feel happy and secure. Also, it is far easier to give more freedoms over time than to take them away once they've been given. Start with limited freedoms and then give more as they learn their boundaries.

Have you used this one yet? "Because I said so, that's why!" Although this isn't the language you want to model, there is truth in this phrase. Don't spend too much time explaining the reasoning behind rules at this stage. A child's conscience doesn't really develop until around age eight, so for now it's enough to do something just because you did indeed say so.

After 25 years of professional and personal experience, I am convinced that what children need are clear, concrete limits with consistent consequences to show them that there is order in the world and a place for them to fit into that. This is what makes a happy and secure child and, consequently, a joyful parent.

### How to Set Limits

There are safety limits, behavioral limits, and language limits. Take one area at a time to focus on while you eventually work towards all the needed areas. Be positive and look at the big picture. It will be a learning process for you both.

**Be positive.** Instead of saying repetitive "no's," try giving "yes" options instead. Teach them not only what they shouldn't do, but what they *should* do. For example, if they are reaching for a vase, say, "That vase is not for you, but you can touch this picture." Or instead of saying, "Don't talk to me that way," try saying "Please ask me in a polite way." Begin your requests with "Would you please..." and end with a "Thank you" just as you would expect them to do.

**Be consistent.** Whether it's a short time of isolation or a firm but gentle warning, set the limit and consequence and then stand by it. One good place to begin is with highchair manners, and then move to physical limits as they begin to be mobile. As they grow in accepting the limits, give them more freedom until at last they can be trusted in any area of your home as well as any other home you enter into.

**Timers are a parents' best friend.** Well, not really, but it caught your attention, right? Use of timers can be very helpful when setting limits that your child can actually measure and see. I like using sand timers, ticking and moving timers, or my favorite, microwave timers because you can literally see the countdown. Use timers to backup instructions like "five more minutes and then time to clean up," "you have ten minutes to put everything back where it belongs," "daddy will be home in one hour," or "twenty more minutes of reading before lights out." In time, your child will get a better sense of what it means when you say "five minutes left" and he will even begin to try to 'beat the clock', which is a pleasant surprise for a parent.

**Here is an example of training from the high chair.** If your child is throwing her cup off the highchair tray onto the ground, hold her hand firmly, make eye contact, and say in a slow and serious voice, "No throwing, please." Then pick up the cup and put it back on the tray and hold her hand again and reiterate the instruction. If she is able, you can even have her repeat the instruction. It's important to anticipate the next throw if she attempts it. Pay close attention and if she starts to throw it again, repeat the rule and keep the cup on the tray if you can. If she does throw it before you can intervene, then just put the cup a distance away and say, "The cup is not for throwing. No more drinking for now." Give the cup back several minutes later and repeat the process. Be aware of power struggles with your child and avoid them if at all possible. If, however, you find that you have entered one, then you must follow-through and outlast your child. Otherwise, your child will know *your* limit and will know how to outlast you in the future.

**Sometimes the reaction a child gets (even if it's that parents are frustrated) reinforces the behavior.** Instead, give her a positive reason to repeat a behavior. For instance, put your hand out towards her cup saying, "May I have it please?" If she doesn't give it to you, guide her hand towards yours and when she puts the cup in your hand say an enthusiastic "thank you!" She'll want to please you and repeat this type of behavior.

If you remain calm, consistent, and positive, the habit of throwing or any other unwanted behavior in the highchair should be altered within a week. Other examples of behaviors that you might want to limit include: blowing raspberries while eating, entering off limit areas of the house, saying "no" inappropriately, or playing rough with other children. Know that you have the right as a parent to set limits with your children and that they want and need it from you.

**Be creative.** Try presenting boundaries in a fresh, new way. For instance, instead of repeated verbal reminders, try using notes to communicate. For instance, one time when I wanted to remind the kids to stay away from the bedrooms while the daycare babies were sleeping, I posted notes on the doors that read, "Thank you for being quiet. I'm sleeping." As they walked by the door and read the note, the children began quietly reminding each other. Even Hope, who could not read at the time, would notice the note and ask what it said. (There's something about a newly posted note that makes everyone want to know the content.) Faith would read it to Hope in a whisper and both would tiptoe away.

**Be repetitive.** It's rare to learn something new the very first time it is introduced. Be patient. When your child fails, give her another immediate opportunity to get it right. Be specific in your expectations and don't assume she knows what you mean. Be very clear and specific and role-play when appropriate.

*Two-year-old Hope was making a habit of screaming any time she wanted something that someone else had. At a time when she had neither the words to express how she felt nor the patience to wait very long, she started to develop this ear-piercing habit. One particular day, little Hope wanted a doll that Grace was playing with. Instead of asking for a turn, she started to grab for the doll while letting out a startling scream. Yes, she was the youngest, and yes, she felt the need to really speak up for herself in a way the other siblings didn't find as necessary, but she also needed to learn a better way to communicate.*

*We pulled her away from the current situation and then set up a re-enactment. We walked her through the process step by step instructing her to refrain from screaming and to use her words. We guided her to patiently say, "Dolly, please?" while waiting for Grace's response. Grace was on to us and knew what we were trying to teach Hope so she hopped right on board and said, "Oh, you want this dolly? When I'm done, I'll give it to you, okay?" Noticing our winks that meant, "Don't make her wait too long," Grace handed over the doll fairly quickly. Then, we said to Hope, "See how Grace will share if you ask nicely? Say, 'thank you, Grace.'"*

As you are committed to walk with your children through this process of accepting limits, be firm, yet understanding. Give ample time for practice and make allowances for mistakes. Never underestimate what children are able to learn, yet be realistic and flexible. The goal is for your children to be a blessing in your home and to all those with whom they come into contact. When children are responsive to instruction, life is more pleasant for all.

## What Type of Tantrum?

Naptime is just minutes away and regardless of how many times your toddler tries to fit that square block into a circular hole it just doesn't fit. As the frustration grows, he finally bursts and throws himself on the ground while flailing his body left and right, screaming so loud you are almost frightened. This is a perfect example of a frustration tantrum. The key here is prevention. Knowing naptime was around the corner and knowing that puzzles can be challenging, it might have been a better choice to read a quiet book or listen to some quiet music to wind down.

On the other hand, there are instances where your child has decided that she is right and refuses to accept your authority. You know that look. You can see it in her eyes. Many parents think they will not be able to distinguish when their child is truly being rebellious but I think your gut will not have you doubting. When you say, "no" and she looks straight at you while still reaching for that forbidden object, she is challenging your authority. If she then drops to the ground and begins the process of accelerating screams and kicking then you know you have a full fledged temper tantrum on your hands. In this case, you need to stand your ground, not give any reinforcing attention to the tantrum, and over time it will become a futile way for your child to get their way. Children are very smart and will not continue in something that is not working for them.

## Watch What You Say

Have you been caught off guard noticing your child saying something they've heard you say? Your children are paying attention to how you talk to them and exactly what you say. Make the most of it and model not only the tone you expect from them, but the attitude behind it. Also, be careful about how you praise. For example, say things like "That was a nice thing to do" and "You must be proud of the good work you did" instead of "You are nice" and "Good girl!" We want our children to know their intrinsic worth separate from their actions. If they are used to hearing you say that they are "good", then when you don't say it, they are apt to interpret the silence as, "Now, I'm a bad person." Their worth should not be based on their actions but who they are as a person. A good person can do bad things and indeed we all do.

When you see unwise choices being made (from your children, others, or yourself), talk to your children about it. Do it with the intent to teach. Discuss how all behavior has consequences with the intent to instill a desire for good. In all cases, extend grace and forgiveness and don't hold grudges or bring up things that should be left in the past. It could be something as simple as saying, "When you touch something that's a no-no, it can break." Said matter-offactly and without anger, the child gets the message that you disapprove of the action, but still love the child.

## Who's Paying Attention to Whom?

Of course you need to be aware of where your children are at all times, but do your children know where you are? When you get out of the car in the mall parking lot, are your children watching to see which way you are going so they can follow you? If you are at the bank, do they look to see when you'll be done at the teller to know when it's time to leave the children's corner? If you chase, they will run. But, instead, teach them to chase after you if you run!

# 12

# "You're My Bestest Friend"

## Sibling Relationships

*When Hope was born, Faith and Grace came to the hospital with a homemade cake for their sister's first BIRTHday! With songs, gift, and photos, it was the beginning of a special sisterhood. In that moment, they were beaming with such a feeling of generosity and togetherness that never could they imagine that a few years down the road they'd be complaining that one of them had slightly more ice cream in their bowl than the others.*

If you believe and teach that siblings are best friends for life, it will be a blessing that carries them throughout their lives and spills out to all those around. Not only will they learn to love within very close proximity, but also it will prepare them to be a faithful friend to those at school, church, and in the scout troops. Ultimately, it will equip them with the skills necessary to have a healthy marriage and prepare them to teach their own children the same truth about the unique gift of sibling relationships.

## Nurturing Sibling Friendships

**When your child is expecting a new sibling, talk to him/her about how this sibling is a gift to them,** specially selected to be their life-long buddy. Have them talk, sing, and read to the baby. Assure your older child that his/her place in the family and in your heart can never be replaced regardless of how many kids are added to the family.

**Encourage and help to plan special gifts and acts of service between siblings,** even in small ways. Here are some examples. When Faith notices that her sisters are running late in the morning, she prepares their toothbrushes and water cups ahead of time for them before leaving the bathroom. One time three-year-old Grace bought five-year-old Faith a box of Macaroni and Cheese with a plastic bowl and fork from the 99¢ store, because that was her favorite meal. It was a simple gesture that Grace could afford, and it had lasting meaning and value. She was so proud to be able to bless her sister in this way.

**Teach your children the difference between tattling and telling.** The first is with the intent to get someone in trouble and the latter is in instances where intervention is necessary for safety. To the dismay of the tattler, try teaching a quick and memorable lesson by applying the consequence to the tattler and not the one being tattled on.

**Don't insist on good behavior before they are ready.** It's okay to *have* negative feelings, but what we *do* with them is what really counts. Give children time and permission to feel, vent, and sort through the feelings so that they can feel 'heard' and then move on to a place where they are able to seek reconciliation on their own.

**Be careful not to label one of your kids** as "the black sheep" or "troublemaker", because if they feel this is how they are seen, they will fulfill that expectation.

**Make a habit of speaking affirmations** towards every member of the family. One of our family traditions is to write special notes of appreciation to each other on holidays like Valentine's Day and Thanksgiving. We read the notes to each other around the dinner table. This tradition is so precious to Grace that she has saved every scrap of paper written to her over the past nine years.

**Treat each child fairly, but not necessarily equally.** What I mean by that is best illustrated in this story following. Here's what you need to know. It was 3:30 p.m. on a Saturday afternoon and the three girls and I were on our seventh errand stop in three hours. Hope got a haircut. Faith got a dress for a play she was in. And, Mommy got in several errands that were all supposed to be "the last one, girls." Because Grace did not acquire any new items that day, she felt very 'left out' and 'unspecial.'

At our last stop, I could see it coming. Seeing Grace's unhappy face, I knew it was time for a big hug and some words of encouragement. "It's sure been a long time out this afternoon, hasn't it?", I say as I draw her in close. She says with her eyes welling up, "Yeah, and Hope gets a haircut and Faith gets a dress and all I got was some fries." I didn't correct her (because her sisters also had gotten ice-cream when she got fries so I know it was even more unfair in her eyes), but just listened with a "Hmm, I see..." I could have opted for a lecture about how I had bought her things whenever she needed them and how she needed to pull herself together and just "get over it," but I could tell what she really needed was empathy and a chance to safely vent to an accepting ear. I also knew that if I had not taken the time to acknowledge and notice her feelings there was a great chance that these feelings would get expressed in inappropriate ways against her innocent sisters.

Don't get me wrong. It was very tempting to go ahead and just do something special for Grace. That would have probably easily stopped her complaining, but I had to stop and realize that would have set a pattern and an expectation for future similar situations. That was something I did not want to do. I had to resist the temptation for a quick solution and reinforce what I'm teaching here.

When we got home Grace tried one last attempt to indirectly influence me to take her for a manicure (something she had been wanting for some time) because she still thought it was only 'fair.' I got down to her level and held her face in my hands and with direct eye contact and a serious, but gentle voice said, "Hope needed a haircut because she had grown her 10 inches for Locks of Love (hair donation program for youth cancer victims) and Faith needed a dress for the Music Man play she is going to be in. Remember that earlier today you said you needed new sharpened pencils for school and didn't I get you those right away? Everyone gets what she needs. If you need anything else, just let me know, okay?"

Life in our household is fair, but not equal. Everyone gets what they need, but they don't necessarily get the same thing at the same time and especially not just because someone else happens to be getting it at the time. What each person gets is different because everyone's needs are different. And, that's okay. In fact, it's a good thing.

So, there is no need to evaluate the size of ice cream scoop that a sister has because like Hope's preschool teacher always said when passing out anything to the class, "You get what you get and you don't throw a fit." And, when your sister gets an award at school, you can and should applaud the loudest because her accomplishment is something to celebrate, whether or not you received the same honor that year. And, finally, when you get a new toy, you are happy to share it because what's more fun than enjoying something with someone you love?

Siblings are best friends who don't compare what they have or don't have. They are happy for each other's accomplishments and feel empathy when others are feeling low. Siblings live life with their siblings through thick and thin and they are there for the long haul. Begin early and nurture the relationship between siblings and you will be laying the foundation for a lifetime.

*Here's a personal illustration of sisters looking out for each other. One day, I told 6-year-old Faith and 4-year-old Grace that after they each finished one page of homework they could go swimming. After about 30 minutes, Grace came up to me and said, "Mommy, mommy, time to go swimming! I did 2 pages of homework. I did one extra so that would count for Faith so we can go swimming now!" Pleased as punch at the loving act towards her sister but trying to explain that each person is responsible for their own work, I told her, "Oh, that is very sweet Gracey, but it really doesn't count." She replied, "But the LOVE counts, right?"*

# 13

# "Now I Know My ABC's"

## Reading & Writing Basics

"ABCB BFG HIJJ MMMOP QRS TUB DUBULOO X
Y IN Z- NOW I KNOW MY ABC'S, NEXT TIME WON'T YOU
THING WITH ME..." *Two-year-old Hope*

This is the process. First, a child learns to comprehend
what you say. Then they learn to speak. Then there's a readiness to
learn to read.  Finally, a child can begin to write. Many parents
teach phonics or writing without consideration of the basics. Comprehension comes first. However, it's often an area overlooked at
home.

Before talking too much about reading and writing, I first want to talk some about speaking and use of sign language:

Q: "When can I start teaching my baby to use sign language and what is the process to teach them this?"

A: Using sign language is such a wonderful way to learn to communicate. As early as you begin speaking to your child verbally, you can use sign language while you speak verbally. Then, as she is old enough to begin to wave, clap, or imitate other gestures, guide your child's hands to follow your signing at appropriate times. He may not produce the signs on his own for another few months but just as you are speaking to him in full sentences and introducing new verbal vocabulary (and repeatedly so...) you can include sign language. It will become a natural part of his communication before you know it and one day he will surprise you and give the sign for "milk" when he is thirsty.

Let's focus on some tips to surround your children with good literature and expose them to a print-rich environment starting as early as age two. Then, the foundation will be laid for your child to learn to read and write.

Q: "What kinds of things can I do to help my child practice the fine motor skills necessary to learn to write? Then, when they are ready, how do I start the process of teaching writing?"

A: Even before your child is physically ready to hold a pencil, practice using a finger to draw lines and circles in sand, a bowl of dry rice, and in water. Make use of the many nursery rhymes that use finger play to act out the songs such as

"The Itsy Bitsy Spider" and "I'm a Little Teapot." Also, give many opportunities to sort, stack, and pick up small objects.

**Later, when your child is showing good small motor control and interest in writing** (age 3-6), begin by tracing practice. Use a large pencil like the Dixon Ticonderoga Pencil with medium soft lead. Teach him his name first with a capital at the beginning and lower case letters afterwards. Some people think lower case letters should be taught later, but since your child will be required to write his name correctly as early as in preschool, it's a good idea to teach him correctly from the start so you do not have to break any bad habits.

**Q:** "What can I do to help expose my child to reading in a fun way?"

**A:** Take sentence strips or lined index cards and write vocabulary words such as "television, table, chair, door," etc. and label your house at eye level. Once they are familiar with these sight words (words they don't have to sound out but they can read by sight), then mix up the cards and put them in the wrong spots. They will enjoy trying to put the cards back on the correct objects.

**Take advantage of city libraries.** There are story times for infants, toddlers, and preschoolers where they can hear stories, sing songs, and make crafts. It's also a great place to meet families with children the same ages. Plan a play date after story time each week!

**Model reading for enjoyment.** Not only do you want to spend time reading with your child but also model reading your own literature. You'll be amazed how powerful this image is to a child when you see them plop down next to you with their own pile of books. This exemplifies teaching by example.

**Write notes to your child.** Children are amused and motivated by notes written specifically to them. Even when they are not able to read, they will enjoy finding the note and having you read it to them. Not only will reading skills be reinforced, but it will be fun, too. Use a dry erase pen to write "Good Morning" on the bathroom mirror or put a small "I love you" note in their lunchbox.

*I used to send notes in four-year-old Grace's lunch boxes and her teachers looked forward to reading them to her every day. One day, she told me it made her feel like school was "homey" because of the daily notes. This added to her sense of security and meant the world to her.*

**Q:** "My son's kindergarten teacher says he needs to know the days of the week and months of the year, but I don't know how to reinforce that in an interesting way. Do you have any ideas?"

**A: Post a calendar** somewhere you will see it often and be referred to. It's most beneficial if they can have a part of putting the calendar together. From preschool through all the elementary grades, your child will master the days of the week, months of the year, as well as understand how to read the date and events on a calendar. This actually helps pre-pare children for reading, as it requires their eyes to track from left to right and move down to the next line.

**There are songs you can sing to teach your child the days of the week.** Try this one to the familiar tune of "Frere Jacques." "Sunday-Monday, Tuesday-Wednesday-Thursday, Friday-Saturday, now we start again. " Check the local library on other songs to teach your children to recite the months of the year as well as their address and phone number. Wee Sing has a fun tape that does this, as well.

Q: "I'm not a natural at teaching and I don't really want to use workbooks with my child. Are there other ways that I can help them to learn?"

A: Expose your child to all the natural wonders of learning all around them. Point out different shapes in traffic signs. Identify colors in buildings, cars, and even the sky. Give them a pad of paper to 'write' a grocery list. Talk about cereal boxes and hand them a coupon to match with the product. Use your creativity and keep your eyes open and the possibilities will prove to be endless.

Q: "I want my child to write thank you cards for gifts that he receives, but he always complains about how tired his hands get. How can I help him?"

A: It's a great idea to get your children in the habit of writing thank you notes. In our house, the rule is: "You can't play with the gift until you write a thank you card." You should see how quickly those cards go out in the mail! Here are a couple of other tricks that can help ensure that your child endures the process of thank you card writing:

1. Use cards preformatted with most of the words needed and with just a few blank lines to fill in for the item re-

ceived and perhaps a word or two about how they will use the item.

2. Take a master of your child's signature to a copy store and make a self-inking stamp. Not only can your child proudly use the stamp on thank you cards, but it is also a wonderful keepsake of your child's first "signature."

As you explore and learn with your children, keep in mind that the process should be in a fun and affirming environment. Encourage curiosity and be excited for your children when they make small discoveries.

*When Grace was 4, she was asking me different math questions like "What is 2+3?" When she was able to figure some out on her own, she was so proud of herself that she'd exclaim, "Hey, Mommy, I'm learning my equals!!"*

## Organizing Projects

As your children begin to produce worksheets and artwork, create a system for handling everything in a way that makes your child feel valued, yet is manageable for you. What we do in our house is hang them with clothespins on a string in the playroom to enjoy for a week or so until new projects are created. Before we re-place old ones, we take a photo and save to put them in scrapbooks so that we will always have a record of their work. With bigger projects like dioramas and relief maps, we take a picture of the child holding the project or take a video to allow the child to talk about the entire process of completing the project.

One day four-year-old Faith was thinking of books she wanted to check out from the library and wanted me to write a list for her. Instead, I had her get a piece of paper and write down the titles herself. She didn't want to do it because she said she didn't know how to write, but I encouraged her to give it a shot anyway. Spelling accuracy was not important. What was most important was that she was communicating through writing. When we got to the library, we were both impressed that she knew that the "CG" she had written meant Curious George. We found the book together and read it with a bit more enthusiasm than we normally would have.

# PART THREE

—

## Five To Ten Years

# 14

# "I Want to See My Money Grow"

### Handling Finances

*One day I saw Hope stacking up a pile of play money with 20's then 10's, 5's, and 1's. Then she neatly placed them in her wallet, which she put carefully into her purse and then hung on the back of a chair. While watching her, I was so impressed with her organization but was curious about where she learned the manner in which she handled her money. When I asked her where she learned to do that, she said, "You, Mommy!"*

**Since actions speak louder than words, model financial priorities.** Instead of limiting yourself to telling them what to do with their money, *show* them and invite them into your process. When you save for purchases or make decisions to buy or not buy, explain to your children the reasoning behind it. Help them understand how to comparison shop, save for big purchases, and avoid debt.

**Give them an allowance and opportunities to earn additional money.** Think carefully about how much you give. It's a personal decision each family needs to make and your decision will vary according to the ages of your children. One rule of thumb is to give the amount that makes them feel they've worked hard to earn it, and yet not too much that they feel they have enough to purchase something right away. You want to develop a work ethic and the ability to set goals and save to meet those goals.

Practically, this is how it looks in our family. We have adapted ideas from Judy Copenbarger to create three categories for our children's earnings: "Save," "Give," and "Spend." Below is a description of each category:

**Save:** A third of their earnings go into a box that cannot be touched, but that they will deposit into a savings account when enough accumulates. When monthly statements come, they can see how their savings have grown. Later, they can use this for gas for the car, books for college, or even for their wedding if it can last that long!

*Two twin four-year-old girls are continually struggling to lift their small heads up high enough to see over the counter at the bank. Their mom is perplexed and a little frustrated; for it is difficult to complete her deposit with the repeated unexplained interruptions. Finally, she leans over and asks them, "What are you trying to see?" They reply in a chant together, "We want to see our money grow!"*

**Give:** A third of their earnings go into this box to be used for birthday gifts or the needs of others. Regular money given to church or other charities comes out of this as well. As children get older and learn to calculate percentages, parents can teach their children to calculate 10% or more but because they have grown accustomed to giving 30%, it will be an easy adjustment. They say people who regularly give are known to be happier than those who don't. This holds true for even the youngest of givers.

*One day, 8-year-old Grace came home and went to her "Give" box and emptied all $24. Then, she proceeded to take some funds out of her "Spend" box (which is her prerogative) so that she could take all $32 to give to an orphanage in India. How great it was that she had already been saving her money so that when an opportunity such as this presented itself, she had the resources to give so generously. As much as I believed in what she was doing, honestly, it was hard for me to see her give away everything she had saved in one fell swoop. Her response completely humbled me. "But, mom, I have everything I need and even more than half of what I want and they don't even have shoes!"*

**Spend:** A third of their earnings go into a box to be used for a pre-determined specific purpose that is saved up for. Some examples are: a special toy or that special outfit that your child has had an eye on, or an outing to a movie with a friend. Later when

your children are older, they can save up for camp or a prom dress and they will be able to put to use these skills learned at an early age.

There are many different ways to handle allowances and teaching our children about financial responsibility. As you adapt and adjust the ways you handle this in your family, keep in mind what's most important: learning the value of money and work.

> While we were walking to the register at the car wash, 4-year-old Hope discovered an adorable stuffed poodle with a carrier that she immediately fell in love with. She looked at the price tag, and then determined to save that amount of money so that she could earn enough to buy herself a pet. From doing extra chores for Grandma (Okay, so Grandma did help a bit more than I expected when she gave $5 for moping the floors!) to saving her allowance at home, Hope was able to save enough within a couple of weeks. I have never seen a child adore a toy as much as Hope did this stuffed poodle. So much more value is placed on an object when it's earned by your own hard work.

# 15

# "What's a Squeegee?"

## Teaching Responsibility

*"I don't want to do any chores, Mommy, because that is your job. And, when I'm all grown up can you come live with me and do them for me?"*

*—an unknown three-year-old child that does not live in our house*

Describe your child at age 25. Are you using words like "responsible," "dependable," and "independent?" If so, what are you actively doing to instill these character traits into your children?

It is very common to find parents doing a bit too much for their children. In an effort to show their love to their children, they end up taking on all the responsibilities of the family, including tasks that should rest on their children's shoulders.

How many times have you seen a trail of clothing in the hall and while complaining out loud to your child, started picking it up yourself? I know it's faster to do it yourself, but will it really be the quicker option if you have to continue to do it for 18 years?

As a general rule, we can all expect and require our children to do more than they are currently doing. Children as young as 12 months old can begin to learn to behave responsibly and see that they need to carry their own weight in the family. Not only does sharing the household responsibilities relieve one person from doing it all, but also it creates a family pride that goes a long way. What a blessing it is when you start seeing even your smallest children noticing and anticipating needs around the house and initiating before even being asked!

Depending on the maturity of your child, tasks might vary by age, but here is a general list to be used as a frame of reference.

**Tasks by Age:**

**One to Two:**
1. Throwing clothes into hamper
2. Wiping down chairs, walls, and doors
3. Throwing things in trash
4. Helping to set the table before meals
5. Cleaning up toys with help
6. Getting items off grocery shelves and into a cart
7. Bringing an item to someone at their request

**Three to Four:**
1. Sorting laundry by color; putting clothing in washer/dryer
2. Matching and folding socks

3. Setting table on own. (Tips: Placemats with a diagram of a table setting can be found at the 99 Cent Store. Keep plates, cups, and utensils in an easily-accessible cabinet.)
4. Clearing table and wiping down table after meals
5. Beginning to hang up and fold clothing
6. Holding open doors
7. Matching coupons to items in the store (Show them to the right aisle and shelf)
8. Changing own clothing with help

**Five to Seven:**
1. Answering the phone and taking messages
2. Folding clothes and putting them away
3. Sweeping/vacuuming and wiping down bathroom counters
4. Setting washer/dryer and dishwasher
5. Peeling carrots, cucumber, and potatoes
6. Taking out trash
7. Ordering own food at restaurants
8. Making grocery lists and finding items at the store
9. Making own bed; changing sheets
10. Getting ready in the morning without help

**Eight to Ten:**
1. Organizing clothes in closet, putting together outfits; shopping for essentials
2. Helping younger siblings with tasks
3. Keeping a calendar of events
4. Following recipes and preparing simple meals: i.e. scrambled eggs, Mac/cheese, grilled cheese, and fruit salad.
5. Cleaning toilets and showers
6. Washing dishes
7. Filling out own paperwork from school (i.e. fills out address/phone/etc. and parents just sign on the dotted line)

8. Doing chores without being asked or reminded
9. Making phone calls and leaving messages

There are many interesting ways to organize your children to help with household chores. The one that works the best for us is the use of index cards. On each card I have one task with a detailed description of what that task entails. Each morning I put out one card for each child (more on the weekends) and when they complete that task they flip the card over to signal that it is done. Then, they come report to either their dad or me to verify completion and satisfaction of task completed.

The reason I like this method is because in our house there isn't always a set day when every task needs to be done, so I like the flexibility of mixing and matching as needed. Also, different children can be assigned different tasks as needed and one child does not always need to do the same chore week after week or month after month.

Here is an example of our "Downstairs Bathroom" chore card:

---

1. Carefully remove all items from counters and floors.
2. Wipe down counter and sink.
3. Windex mirrors.
4. Mop floor, especially all around toilet area.
5. Wipe down toilet inside and then get mom to help with scrubbing inside last.
6. Wash hands with soap.
7. Replace all items on floor and counters.
8. Flip chore card over and report to mom or dad.

---

Some other methods that might work well for other families include giving the same tasks (i.e. vacuuming, dusting, polishing) to one child for an entire quarter, then rotating jobs by the quarter. Or, you can post a calendar with a schedule of daily tasks that need to be done.

Whatever the method, find what works for you and your family and stick with it. Remember to turn on the tunes and whistle while you work!

**Use pictures.** Sometimes parents have a clear idea of expectations, but children don't naturally share the same understanding. To clearly communicate and be on the same page about what is expected, take a picture of a clean room or a made bed and post it so your child can refer to the picture. Take the photo down once the reminder is no longer needed.

**Sometimes you might find the need to work harder to reinforce one particular responsibility.** In that case, consider using a short-term (2-3 cycles max) solution in the form of a behavior chart (see appendix). Although you don't want to rely on this method to teach all behaviors, it can come in handy to get a child over a particular hurdle at one point in time. For instance, you may find your child needing some extra motivation to: finish their morning routine before the timer goes off, stay in bed all night long, start on their chores before being asked, or putting their clothes in the hamper each day. Depending on the age of the child, you might set a week-long or month-long goal (the younger, the shorter the goal) and together determine a positive reinforcer when they have consistently accomplished their goal. When you get to this point, be sure to emphasize that it's been your child's accomplishment and not the parents'. If your child finds pride in their accomplishment, they will naturally not look to outside means to keep them on track in this area anymore, so plan on doing away with the chart as soon as you see sufficient progress. (See appendix for helpful incentive charts that you can personalize and tailor to your needs.)

# 16

# "Just Mom and Dad and Me"

## One-on-One Time

The last year I taught third grade, I decided I was going to take out each of my children out for lunch for their birthday. I organized groups of students by birthday months and walked with them to the nearby fast food restaurant for lunch and conversation. The results were amazing.

My initial purpose was to help my students feel recognized and to know of their value to me. What I didn't expect was that it would significantly reduce the need for discipline in my class. As trust was built into each teacher-student relationship, a deeply shared respect was nurtured. Our short but meaningful time together at lunch served to build a trust that was significant. The importance of connecting one-on-one with students really hit home that year.

Likewise, one-on-one time with each of our children serves a great purpose. It's something children desire and need and they will do whatever it takes to get that time. To demonstrate this, let me share the story of when Grace was 18 months old.

*I was out on a quick errand and after a long, hard day at work, my husband was keeping an eye on Grace while resting on the couch. (Some of you can already see where this is going.) When I returned from my shopping, I found my husband asleep out on the couch! Now, what surprised and touched me the most was what Grace was doing beside him. In an effort to be near him and wanting to feel connected, she had used his chest as a table for her tea party. With a full setting precariously balanced on his chest with each rise and fall, she was carefully sipping and having a quiet little conversation so as not to disturb his sleep.*

## Quality Time

Everyone talks about 'quality time', but how can you be assured that the time you set aside will actually be of a certain quality? There really is no way to assure this. For example, let's say you plan to go out to dinner with your son alone and you excitedly come to the time with a list of topics to cover. You bring up one subject at a time and you are met with comments like, "I don't know" or "I guess so." Your dreams of "quality time" are not realized even though you had set aside this time with the hope that your relationship would reach new depths.

Quality of relating comes from being there and being there a lot. It's hard to predict when your child will feel like opening up or when an important moment is just around the corner. The only way to insure that you will catch precious moments is to be present a large percentage of the time. Be alert to the possibilities and be avail-able when the time is ripe.

Both my husband and I have made a decision to be actively in our children's presence on a consistent and prominent basis. I am a stay-at-home mom first, then a daycare provider and consultant. In fact, I have worked my career around my priority of family. My husband has also intentionally chosen to work in the elementary schools because that schedule coordinates with our children and he can work full-time in a profession he loves, yet be home at 4 p.m. as well as all school holidays and summers. We also decided to move closer to his work so that we can enjoy breakfasts together as well as reduce his commute time and be closer to grandparents. Along the journey, there were many opportunities to make other choices in regards to career. Because of our shared priority to be together as a family, we have stayed committed to the choices we have made.

The details of your family will look different, but be creative and open to new possibilities that will allow you to be present with your family in new and exciting ways. Perhaps you can carpool to work, thereby saving time on the road and getting home earlier to be with family. Go ahead and use those vacation days and whisk your family away on that much-needed trip away. Consider planning more family oriented events at work so that your loved ones can meet those with whom you work. How about a "Bring Your Daughter to Work Day?" Might it even be possible to take a day off to honor your child on their birthday and spend a day doing whatever he wants? Whatever you decide, your efforts towards more family time will not be in vain.

In addition to making time together a priority, both my husband and I have worked routine one-on-one times into our weekly schedule so that each child gets each parent's undivided attention for at least an hour and sometimes a whole afternoon. To simplify and insure that this happens, we integrate time with each child into the weekly schedule we already have in place. For instance, we intentionally have my husband drive Faith back and forth from violin lessons each week so they can have weekly car chats. When time allows, they extend that afternoon for more quality time. My one-on-one time with Hope is the first hour of my daycare babies' naps on Tuesdays. We chat, do puzzles, color, read books, and bake together. My time with Grace is every Saturday at 2 p.m. If we are out on a family outing, we'll be sure to steal away together for some uninterrupted time together. With Faith approaching the 'tween years', I have begun working through a series of mommy and daughter dates with her. Check out the *Secret Keeper Girl* set by Dannah Gresh.

Hop on aboard these crucial years of interactions as we only get one shot at them. You will not only deepen your relationship with your children, but with each twist and turn, there will be unexpected wonders day by day.

### What Do I Say?"

Reach out and connect. Avoid questions like, "How was your day?" Or "Did you have a good day?" but instead, ask things like, "Who did you play with at recess?" or "What book did you choose from the library?" These types of questions are less likely to produce answers like, "Fine" or "Yes" and may open up avenues for longer, more significant sharing. Another idea is to share stories of when you were the age of your children. My kids are always asking for more of this type of sharing.

# 17

# "Can Grace
# Come Out and Play?"

## Friendships and Reaching Out

*Each of our children used to invite a friend to dinner every Wednesday night. This would serve many purposes. First, it would bless the friends by giving them a taste of family life that they didn't necessarily have at home. Secondly, it would provide our children relational time with friends that would enhance family time, not take from it. Third, it would give us insight into our children's friendships in a way that provided interesting topics to discuss later. But, mainly, it would be fun!*

So much joy is missed when a family keeps to itself and doesn't look beyond the four walls of their own home. As families reach out to others, blessings beyond measure can be discovered.

Sometimes it's fine to go with the flow, but not in the area of your children's social life. Be an intentional influence. Don't send your child to others' homes just because it's easy. Parents learn much more when their children's friends are in their own home. Invite friends to family events, to join the scout troops, or to come to a church potluck. In short, be active and present in your children's relationships with their friends. It will prove to be valuable for you and all your family.

Including friends in your family time provides many opportunities to continue to reach out and serve. As you learn about needs, plan with your children ways that you can be a blessing. Perhaps a friend needs a ride to school or you find that they could accompany you after school and work together on homework.

Extend from there and mow the lawn for a neighbor or bake cookies for the family across the street. If you keep your eyes open, opportunities to reach out will never be scarce.

*When Grace was in first grade, her friend was telling her about a fight her parents had had the previous night. She was telling Grace that her parents were so mad and that her dad ended up leaving the house and saying he'd never come back. After empathetically listening and supporting her friend, Grace came up with these words that she had heard should be said in a situation like this. "Don't worry, honey. And just remember, it's not your fault." I'm not sure if this had any impact on the friend at the time, but I'm hoping and trusting that this comforting truth will come back to her in times that she most needs to hear it.*

# 18

# "Mommy, Why is Steam Coming Out of Your Ears?"

## Handling Anger

*"I feel...when you...because...I want..." When children are feeling at a loss, use this tool to help them work through their anger to get to a peaceful solution. For example, if a sibling grabs a toy from her, she can say, "I feel angry when you grab something from me because I wasn't done playing with it. I want you to ask me next time and wait until I'm done."*

### Looking at Ourselves

We've all seen it. Maybe it was us. That lady in the store who is yelling at her kids and those around are thinking, "Wow, that mom really needs to get a handle." From a distance we know clearly what is good or right, but when we are in the thick of it, everything is quite muddy.

We've all done it. We feel angry and we respond in a way that causes us remorse. It's normal and yes, it's forgivable, but it is also true that your children are watching and learning all the time, whether you want them to or not. If you are concerned about their outbursts then perhaps consider turning the mirror the other way and examining your own responses. Are you shouting at your kids to stop shouting? What do you think you are really communicating?

## Ways to Reduce Risk of Angry Outbursts

**Slooooow down.** No one is chasing you. It's okay to not finish the laundry. You have the right to have a quiet moment by your-self. Take a coffee break, take a nap, get a manicure.

**Just say "No!"** Not to drugs, well, okay to drugs, but also to requests for time commitments. Just because it's a "good" thing doesn't mean you have to do it. Sometimes it's a choice between two good options, but sometimes it's a choice for your sanity. A peaceful and happy parent brings much more joy to the journey than one more team sport or another Wednesday night PTA meeting. (Don't tell my PTA I said that!)

**Take a break.** Regularly schedule in things that renew and refresh you like walks on the beach, journaling on a park bench, slowly sipping coffee, and walking the dog. The world will come to an end one day, but it won't be because you decided to put yourself first for once.

**Express Yourself.** Often times, parents rush through life without taking stock of how they might be feeling about something. For instance, you are angry about a hurtful remark someone made to you, but you smiled through it. Later, you might find yourself over-reacting to an innocent spill at the kitchen table.

**Forgive.** You may think you are punishing the one you have a grudge against, but the truth is that it rests with you. Your health and happiness are at risk if you are holding onto that poison. Let it go...

## Looking at Our Children

Sometimes parents say things like, "Oh, he's just an angry child," or "He has his father's temperament" as a way of excusing angry behavior. Yes, it's okay to be angry, but there are limits to what is an acceptable expression of anger. What's important is to deter-mine the root of the emotions.

## Possible Reasons for Anger in Your Children

**There has been a change in their routine.** Have you recently moved? Is Dad on a business trip? Did your child not get their daily outlet of physical activity? Does your child have a long-term substitute teacher at school? Or perhaps there has been more activity than usual and she has not been getting a good night's rest. Talk to your child and ask questions like "What would make you feel better?" or begin a conversation with the statement "Things just haven't been the same around here, have they?"

**They are looking for attention.** When a child lacks attention, they will opt for any kind, even negative. When was the last time you really sat down and completely focused on your child and what they were interested in? Make plans to be actively present with your child for the next few weeks and see how it makes a difference. See chapter 16 for more encouragements in this area.

**They are not being heard.** It feels terrible when another person does not receive your words. Take stock in the last few days of conversations and see if you can pinpoint a time when your child seemed frustrated or defensive. Or find out if there has been a situation with a teacher, friend, or sibling.

**They are rejecting your limits.** Especially when setting limits is a new event in your home, you can expect to find some resistance. Sometimes anger is used to mask the fact that children just don't want to be instructed. Stay consistent, be fair, but be open to evaluating this part of your parenting if necessary.

**They don't know!** Understanding emotions is complicated. Even the most intelligent adults react in anger and do not fully understand the root of their feelings. Until you can help them figure what is at the source of the anger, allow them time to vent. Accept and validate their feelings. Listen intently without correction or evaluation of their feelings. You can put limits on how they express their anger (i.e. "Use words, not your body."), but if they feel your support, you're well on your way to resolving the problem.

**Sometimes a "time out" is needed.** Not the type where you sit on a small chair and face the wall as a punishment, but the type where you take time out of the current situation to get calm. It's okay to be angry, but children need safe and acceptable ways to work it out. If your child is more physical by nature, try using play-doh, a punching bag, or a pillow. Provide guidelines such as allowing them to hit the pillow, but not throwing it at people or stopping an activity if it doesn't seem to be helping. After he is calmer, he will be much more likely to reasonably work towards a solution. If your child is more verbal or enjoys drawing, try letting her express her feelings through drawing, scribbling, or writing. Sometimes, this sufficiently releases the negative feelings so that she can move on. Other times, it will help reveal what is at the root of her feelings and you can go from there.

**Enjoy the Ride**

One time one of our daughters was just beside herself with emotion when she felt misunderstood by one of her sisters. She was starting to work out her anger inappropriately so we pulled her aside and had her sit down with paper and a pencil and we told her to draw what she was feeling. The first paper had dark, out-of-control scribbling. At that point we validated her feelings with words that she did not have herself. The second paper had lighter scribbles with a bit more form. It was obvious she was still angry, but still not ready to talk. We reassured her that we would help her through her feelings. The third paper was words describing how she was feeling. This provided a start for a two-way conversation. Eventually, we were able to move onto writing about possible solutions. Finally, she decided to write letters to her sisters to express her feelings, but also to apologize for her part in the conflict. The whole process took about 45 minutes.

As you begin to examine your own responses to situations and begin the process of expressing anger in productive and appropriate ways, have your children walk alongside you. One idea is to write a list of acceptable and unacceptable ways to express anger. For instance, it is okay to take a break, cry, talk, write, or listen to music. It is not okay to yell or use your body to express how you feel. Post the list in a place where anyone can take a breather from a tense situation and have time to evaluate and plan their course of action. Of course we want to handle things better overall, but remember that, in the end, we are all human and are bound to fall short. Be patient, forgiving, and understanding.

# 19

# "Ticket for Two"

## Self-Care

Saturday night is date night. The girls love their teenage sitter and the feeling is mutual. Dave and I play tennis, ride bikes, take walks or go to dinner and a movie. It is a wonderful time to connect weekly, and it has brought so much life into our marriage. Sometimes, however, I have to admit, there are bumps in the road. As much as we'd like every date night to be sweet and wonderful, there are times when the time is spent resolving conflict. As we are tempted to complain about the fact that we are paying a babysitter to have time to have our "heavy discussion," we realize that even this time is precious. Consider the alternative: being at home in the presence of the children and being tempted to push aside an issue that needs to be addressed. Date night is always a blessing.

**We are all human, and it's healthy for children to see their parents as such.** When you're sad, cry. When you're angry, say so, but act with integrity. When you're worried, show them how to find peace. And, please, when you make a mistake, admit it and ask for forgiveness. Children cannot be expected to do what they have not experienced themselves.

**In the same way, children need to learn about self-care by your example.** How will your child know its importance if they don't see it modeled by their parents? I know it can feel like neglecting your child if you take time out for yourself, but this couldn't be further from the truth. When you take time to do the things that enrich your life, then your children indirectly benefit from it as well. And, as you are rejuvenated, you can continue to give wholeheartedly to your family. So, if you're not going to do it for yourself, do it for your children!

## Self-Care Suggestions

**Set up a babysitting co-op.** When Faith was just a few months old, my husband and I decided to trade babysitting on a biweekly basis with two other families with newborns the same age. Each couple would watch all three babies at one time and then get to go out the following two times while the other couples rotated in. To be honest, after four hours with three small infants my husband and I would wonder what we got ourselves into, but then when it was our turn to go out, we had no doubt it was a good thing!

**Nurture your interests and hobbies.** There are few things more exciting then to learn something new and fun. Try a sewing course at a local community college or join a bowling league. Whatever it is that you do, jump in with both feet and enjoy!

**Take regular annual vacations separate from family trips.** You know what they say: When you go with your kids, it's a trip.

When you go alone or with your spouse, then it's a vacation! It doesn't have to be an exotic location (although you won't find me complaining if my husband suggests Hawaii), but the main point is to get away. Take the time to reflect on the past, enjoy the present, and plan for the future. Look at personal goals, marriage goals, family goals, and financial goals. You'll return to normal life refreshed and with newfound perspective and purpose. When you return home, you will find that everyone is happier.

**Sleep, eat, and exercise.** Sounds simple and basic and it is. Plan healthy menus, get to bed early, and work in exercise routines. When you feel good, it will rub off onto everyone else in your family. You set the tone in your family so make it a melodic one.

There's so much more to good parenting than acquiring parenting techniques. When parents take care of themselves in a way that honors their lives, then the benefits overflow onto the entire family. Don't ever feel guilty about taking care of yourself first. Everyone in the family benefits from a mom or dad who is happy and healthy first.

# 20

# "A Little of This and a Bit of That"

## Miscellaneous Tips and Quotable Quotes

### Martyn Manners

How many times have you told your children to "keep their elbows off the table" or "chew with their mouths closed?" Too many to count, right? Each time it gets more and more frustrating, and we wonder when we will ever be able to have a peaceful meal together.

We need to remember that mealtime manners are the responsibility of each person. To help with this, I decided to write up our "Martyn Family Manners" to post on the wall in our kitchen for all to refer to. After saying grace, we would all look at the list of manners to refresh our memories. Then while eating we were able to give gentle reminders like, "Number 3" instead of the constant nagging that had been taking place. The kids were also able to look up at the list and remind themselves throughout the course of the meal. After several weeks with this list, most of the manners had become natural routine at the table and we were able to take it down. Of course, not every meal was perfection, but the quality of the time together greatly improved.

---

### Martyn Manners

1. Be thankful for another meal.
2. Arrive at the table with clean HANDS and no toys.
3. Chew with mouth closed & speak with an empty mouth.
4. Keep your elbows off the table and sit straight.
5. Finish minimum requirement (milk, veggies)
6. ASK about someone else's day.
7. Tell about your day.
8. Wipe your face and hands on napkins every few bites.
9. Thank the cook and wait until everyone is done.
10. Clear the table and floor.

---

One fun mealtime activity that we've used around the table is a version of the well-known game "Two Truths and a Lie." This is how it works: Each person tells three things about his/her day, two of which actually did happen and one that didn't. Then, the guests around the table guess which is the "lie."

When our family plays this game not only does each person excitedly participate, but everyone feels validated and listened to, which encourages follow up questions and happy and peaceful subsequent mealtimes. Try taking this model and adapting it to share about other areas such as "Christmas Wishes," "Lifetime Dreams," "Vacation Destinations," etc. The possibilities are endless!

## Funny Moments Around the Dinner Table

*We hear a faint but very distinguishable sound that comes with a very distinctive odor. A moment later, we hear, "Umm...excuse me, but my bottom burped."*

*Three-year-old Hope notices that we are having a different kind of rice and she asks what type it is. I tell her it's Jasmine rice and without even a moment to process she belts out, "A whole new rice!"*

*Four-year-old Hope's rendition of a well-known prayer at mealtime:*
*God is great*
*God is nice*
*I love the food*
*I love rice*
*Thank you God for all this food*
*I love you, you're my dude.*

## Teething

Around eight months, those first teeth start to emerge. How-ever, don't be surprised if it happens much later or earlier. Some babies are even born with teeth! (see appendix for Tooth Eruption Schedule) Don't be surprised if your baby is uncomfort-able for even a couple months before you see any sign of teeth. It's not uncommon to one day see a tooth pop out and then realize that is the reason baby has been fussy and waking at night. Try refriger-ated rings for teething, gum massage, or rubbery toys to soothe symptoms.

### Early Mornings

If you have a very early morning and don't want to hassle with rousing a child from deep sleep and getting them dressed, consider this option. Put them to bed in their street clothes. Choose something comfortable and that doesn't wrinkle. In the morning, strap your drowsy child into his car seat and then hit the road. When you get to your destination, your child will have had time to adjust to the morning. With a quick freshening up, he will be ready for the day.

### Modeling

During your annual get-away, take time to evaluate areas of challenge for each of your children. I like to bring my children's journals with me. I read the past year's New Year's resolutions to celebrate their growth as well as considering new goals for the year. Often times, my husband and I have realized that a particular area of challenge mirrors some area in our own lives that needs improvement. This has challenged us to be more intentional about modeling health in all areas of our lives that would spur our children onto growth as well. For instance, one year seven-year-old Faith was really struggling in her ability to accurately describe less familiar objects around the house and neighborhood. I couldn't understand why it was such a struggle for her until one day, I told her to hand me the "thingamabob." The realization that we shared this area of weakness hit me like a ton of bricks. From that day on, I became very, you know, doing it on purpose and not making mistakes and stuff and modeling really good talking.

### Individuality

How is it that children from the same parents can be so different? In fact, isn't it often the case that siblings can have opposite type personalities? Given this fact, it's very important for parents to take into consideration the individuality of each child. Yes, the standards should remain the same, but there is much room for how everything plays out according to a child's temperament, personality, strengths, and weaknesses. Also, while you want to accept each child as they are, be careful not to be an "enabler" in their weaknesses. Aim to accept, but guide towards growth. For example, Grace has always been our most shy child. While we wouldn't encourage her to run for student body President, when it comes to greeting friends and neighbors, we do require her to wave or smile because it's just plain good manners.

## Fill Me Up

What fills your emotional tank? For some, it's quality one-on-one time with someone. For others it's a quiet walk in the park alone or a big party with lots of new people. For some it's receiving a note or gift or a big hug! Figure out what feeds your child and then regularly tank them up! If you do, chances are very high that you will have a content child who will feel less of a need to act out for attention and will be overall much more cooperative and helpful.

## Serving Together

Instead of just telling our children to reach out to others and serve, we make plans and do it together. It's especially fulfilling to reach out beyond the close circle of friends that we share. Especially around the holidays, but at other times during the year, our family schedules times to serve together. We've sung carols and passed out gifts at homeless shelters, convalescent homes, and neighbor's homes. As the children grow older, they grow in taking bigger parts in planning and execution. Often, they are the initiators and involve others in the family.

# Epilogue
## Last Stop?

This is the end, but it is also just the beginning. As you are now equipped with tools to handle many crucial parenting issues, may you find freedom in that. As the nitty gritty of parenting no longer overwhelms you, may you find time and energy to explore more of the journey that was before, perhaps, out of reach. Or never even in the realm of possibilities. Perhaps you'll discover that you have a passion for watercolor, an inclination towards cross-country skiing, or a dream to live abroad. Discover it, embrace it, and receive it as an invitation to another leg of the journey.

Remember to not only embrace the entire journey, but also the whole child. Look beyond the skills that need to be taught. See the heart. Look deeply into the eyes of your children. See the needs. Walk alongside your children and vision together. See their future. Accept, encourage, and dream together.

*As Grace's fourth birthday was quickly approaching, we had this casual conversation over lunch one day:*

**Mom** *"The 4th of July is coming, but your day is coming too and that's more special."*

**Grace** *"I'm MORE special???!!!!"*

**Mom** *"Of course you are!"*

*Later that evening, we were having a quiet moment by her bedside and it was obvious it had been on her mind all day. Here's how the conversation continued:*

> **Grace** *"Am I so special??"*
> **Mom** *"Of course, you are very special– to me, to daddy, to sister and most of all to God."*
> **Grace** *"Yeah, even my bad stuffs are special..."*

As you continue on your journey of parenthood, remember the unique wonder of each child. Affirm each child for who he is and who he has yet to become. Dream big dreams for your children and allow them to dream for themselves. Give ample time for growth and change, because you know that nothing good we do comes easily.

Above all, embrace the entire package of parenting. Learn to see the good in all the challenges and grow from them. Savor each moment, even the 'bad stuffs', because joy comes through each part of this glorious journey of parenthood.

*It's 7 a.m. on day seven of our California road trip and the temperature outside reads 77 degrees. Tired but happy souls head out to the parking lot with our morning song, "O Happy Day" calling out to us from the car stereo. Sweet memories fill our heads. We reminisce about eating root beer flavored licorice on Route 66, sneaking through a ghost town, searching for Astro Burger on Hwy 139, and climbing Mount Whitney after a slice of nacho chorizo pizza (okay, so it was our car doing the climbing...). We happily continue on in our journey as four-year-old Hope asks, "Mommy, where are we going next on our BIG field trip?" As we anticipate the songs, stories, laughs, and the Dennis the Menace playground just miles away, we are enjoying the ride.*

Thank for sharing in the journey of parenting.

Here's to the rest of the ride.

Enjoy!

# Resources

**MORE RESOURCES AND GREAT IDEAS AT**
**www.MothersFriendSOS.com**

# Enjoy the Ride

# How To Use These Resources

You can find electronic versions of these and many more charts and resources (which you can customize to fit your own needs) at our website, www.mothersfriendsos.com.

## INCENTIVE CHARTS

**As you use the incentive charts, carefully consider rewards and consequences. Remember** that the main goal of using such interventions is that your child would become self-motivated and independent in monitoring his own progress. The charts are meant to be that extra boost needed for a short period of time, but one day the charts should not be necessary. If effective, eventually your child will look at the chart and say on his own, "Oh! I don't need that anymore!"

**If you have a non-reader,** use pictures or drawings to identify tasks or skills on a chart. For instance, if her morning routine includes brushing her teeth, then draw a picture of a toothbrush next to that task so that she can 'read' the chart on her own.

## REWARDS

**The primary award of successfully completing a chart is your child's satisfaction, growing independence, and responsibility.** So, think carefully about rewards during and at the completion of charts. Feel free to use stickers during the process, but keep it simple; no big prizes each day or too frequently along the way. Have your child do the monitoring, putting on stickers, etc. Use words of encouragement and hugs to keep up momentum, but keep your child's focus on their own sense of satisfaction and accomplishment. Avoid threats and bribes, although I know its tempting to want to give a crisp hundred dollar bill to the first child who cleans their room and comes down to dinner.

**The reward at the end of the week or month (depending on your child's age) should be something related to what's been learned.** For instance, at the end of the learning period of a chore chart, perhaps you can go out together and purchase a fun apron to use while cooking for the family. Or, once your child becomes efficient at remembering to do their morning routine without reminder, you can go shopping together for a new backpack for school. Rewards should reinforce the skill being learned and not be a goal
in and of themselves. So, no Disneyland trips for doing homework and no new bikes for doing chores!

**Here's to having happy and independent children** who have pride in their own accomplishments as well as what they can contribute to the family unit! Enjoy!

**What you need (and don't need) on your**

# Baby Registry

*There is such a plethora of items available and I know it can be very overwhelming. There will be choices that you will want to make according to your taste for style/color, etc but this list includes those items that, in my opinion, are the essentials. You will find some items listed generically and others with particular brands. The latter was determined by personal experience and/or consumer reviews and are considered superior choices. Always confirm these choices with your own evaluation/needs. Some things (like carseats and diaperbags) you just need to have new, but there are many items that it just makes more sense to borrow or buy second hand. The latter category is indicated with an asterisk(\*) after the item.*

❑ **Carseat** Britax carseat has been determined to be the best, but I recommend moving to this after 20 lbs. In the first few months it is very convenient to have an infant in a carseat that can easily be removed from car.

❑ **Carseat insert\*** With neck muscles still developing, a newborn needs this extra support for their head. Also provides a more secure fit for the body. As they grow it changes with them. Make sure to have the security strap for use when rear-facing.

❑ **Bassinet\*** Try to borrow one if possible (since you'll only use it for about 3 months) or use the top of a pack 'n play.

❑ **Contour changing pad\*** Instead of getting a changing table that will ultimately be a useless piece of furniture, I would highly recommend getting a dresser and putting a pad on top of the dresser. Later you can remove the pad and store books/pictures, etc.

❑ **Stroller\*** It's nice to have the type where you can transfer baby still in carseat. Also consider weight, easy fold, and space in basket underneath.

❑ **BJÖRN baby carrier\*** Great for back support and comes in larger sizes for tall daddies; also "Active" model has extra lumbar support.

❑ **Ergo carrier\*** For those with back trouble, this is the carrier of choice. Can be bought at myfavoritebabycarrier.com.

❑ **Convertible high chair\*** Get the kind that attaches to chairs and can be used even when child grows. The last thing you need is a bulky piece of furniture.

❑ **Blankets** Have many thicknesses and sizes on hand. My favorite are thin knitted ones and the big ones from Gymboree.

❑ **Infant seat\*** Very useful not only for playing but also the first month of feeding solids.

❑ **Bathtub\*** Consider ones that convert to bathchair and have their own water sprayer. The SUMMER brand has a good one.

❑ **Thermometer** Ear or temporal scanners are nice and quick.

❑ **Video baby monitor\*** You can see your baby's face even in the dark. Useful early on and when baby moves from crib to bed and beyond. Keep sound dial ow as it really magnifies sound. I recommend the Summer brand.

❑ **Digital baby monitor** If you find static to be a problem, try a digital monitor.

❑ **Crib\*** Avoid really fluffy and cushiony items around baby until they can move around well on their own. (min 4 mo)

❑ **Mattress pad** You'll need at least two of these. Waterproof.

❑ **Sheets\*** You'll need 2-3 sets of these.

❑ **Bumper\*** Keeps baby from getting caught in crib railing or bumping their head. Again, video monitor comes in handy here so you can not only hear, but see that baby is safe.

## CLOTHING

❑ **Onesies\*** Easy one-piece suits to go under clothing or worn as an outfit. 5-7.

❑ **Drawstring buntings\*** Get the kind that closes at the bottom or baby's feet will fall out.

❑ **Sleep sac\*** Babies won't keep blankets on when sleeping. This will help.

❑ **Footed clothing/pj's\*** Get the kind that zips. Avoid buttons and snaps.

❑ **Socks\*** Find ones with elastic around ankles or they will never stay on.

❑ **Hats\*** Especially important for those Winter babies. Get knit ones.

## CONSUMABLE

❑ **Diapers/wipes** You'll need newborn sizes for only the first 2-4wks. Plan on using 10-12 a day. For days until umbilical cord falls off, use ones with slit. You'll need a smaller refillable package for your diaper bag, one for the car, and one for home.

❑ **Rash cream** My favorite is Butt Paste. You won't forget this name.

❑ **Shampoo** I suggest you get a kit that includes everything- cleanser, clippers, etc.

❑ **Medicines** Again, here, kits are good.

# NURSING MOMS

❑ **Double breast pump** I recommend MEDELA brand. New recommendation is not to share pumps.

❑ **Milk storage bags** Doubled lined/'ziploc' style. See breastfeeding chapter 2 for tips on pumping and storing milk.

❑ **Lansinoh breast cream** Won't hurt baby, but try to use 1 hour before nursing and air dry.

❑ **Nursing pads** You'll need these everyday for the first several weeks so stock up!

❑ **Nursing bra** Personally I prefer the ones with the 3 hooks on each side. I recommend that you use the hooks to identify which breast you will need to begin nursing on at each feeding.

# LATER  (after first 6 mos)

☐ **Exersaucer/walker\*** begin at 4-6 mos. don't use for more than 30 min at a time. Has been known to affect forming of legs.

☐ **Jumper\*** begin at 6-8 mos

☐ **Bedrail\*** useful for when moving from crib to bed

☐ **Cups/utensils/bowls** around 4-6 mos when feeding solids; nice to get some travel ones to keep in diaper bag. For very fussy babies who don't seem to take to any sippy cups, try the type with open spout (no insert) or drink straight from a soft rim.

# OPTIONAL

☐ **Pack 'n play\*** very useful for grandma's house or trips

☐ **Nursing coverup\*** Some babies are particular or a blanket can work just as well.

☐ **Changing table\*** \*See note on contour mat above

☐ **Stuffed animals/toys\*** There are great items to borrow but you will probably get a lot of these at your shower whether you register for them or not. They don't need much the first 3 months.

☐ **Glider/rocker\*** Great item to borrow or buy second hand.  Footrest very useful.

☐ **Diaper pail\*** Doesn't cover odor and is hard to unload.  Small plastic bags work just as well.

**Enjoy the Ride**

☐ **Gates*** Don't rely on any safety item to prevent accidents. Babies as young as 6 mos can begin to respond to limits.

☐ **Sling*** Some moms prefer slings over other carriers. Nursing can be done privately as well.

☐ **Mustela sunscreen** Gentle on baby's face and body.

☐ **Swing/rocker** If you use one I suggest using it only for times of high fussiness where nothing else works. Don't let it become a babysitter or a crutch for falling asleep.

☐ **Diaper warmers** Unless your baby is hyper sensitive or it's a very cold Winter, you will not need this.

☐ **Diaper stacker** Instead, get a basket that will hold diapers, wipes, rubbing alcohol, cotton balls, etc.

☐ **Mitts** to protect baby from scratching himself

☐ **Pacifier** okay to use first 3 months, but wean shortly afterwards. Once the teeth start coming in and habits set in, it will be harder to break this attachment so plan to end it early. I like the pacifier with caps. Avent has nice ones but your baby will determine which he prefers.

# Infant Feeding Log

**Date:** _____

| Time feed-ing began | Time since last feed-ing | Duration (if breast-feeding) | | Amount (if bottle feeding) | Wet Diapers | Dirty Diapers | Sleep Hr:min |
|---|---|---|---|---|---|---|---|
| | | R | L | oz. | | | |
| | | R | L | oz. | | | |
| | | R | L | oz. | | | |
| | | R | L | oz. | | | |
| | | R | L | oz. | | | |
| | | R | L | oz. | | | |
| | | R | L | oz. | | | |
| | | R | L | oz. | | | |
| | | R | L | oz. | | | |
| | totals: | | | oz. | | | |

# Introducing Solids

This chart is designed as a quick-reference summary of the information presented in chapter 6.

Remember to avoid these foods during the first year: cow's milk, hot dogs, grapes, popcorn, honey, nuts and peanut butter, and egg whites.

Consult with your doctor as to when to begin introducing solids. If you continue to exclusively breastfeed after 6 months, ask your doctor whether it would be advantageous to use vitamin supplement drops.

| Foods | Notes |
|---|---|
| **4-6 months** | |
| Rice, oatmeal, barley, mixed cereal with breast milk or formula. | Introduce one food at a time, 3-5 days apart to check for allergies. |
| **6-7 months** | |
| Veggies, (green first) Juice- pear or white grape preferred. | Cereal at every meal Maximum 4 oz of juice. |
| **8-9 months** | |
| Cereal puffs/Cheerios, wheat grain breads Yogurt, cheese, tofu, egg yolk, meat, tomato, citrus. | Begin pincher grasp Ignore/deemphasize inappropriate behavior |
| **10-11 months** | |
| Eating most table foods with family 3 times a day. One milk-only feeding. | Reward good table manners Increase self-feeding |
| **12-14 months** | |
| Cow's milk, Orange juice | Wean from bottle; Water only if child wants bottle. |

# Mealtime Manners

1. Be **THANKFUL** for another meal.

2. Arrive at the table with clean **HANDS** and no toys.

3. Chew with your **MOUTH CLOSED** & speak with empty mouth.

4. Keep your **ELBOWS** off the table and sit straight.

5. **FINISH** minimum requirement (milk, veggies)

6. **ASK** about someone else's day.

7. **TELL** about your day.

8. **WIPE** your face and hands on a napkin every few bites.

9. **THANK** the cook and wait until everyone is done.

10. **CLEAR** the table and floor

We've created a colorful and attractive Mealtime Manners placemat. You can see it (and purchase it) at www.MothersFriendsos.com.

# Behavior Chart for     week of:

| Using Manners | Mon | Tues | Wed | Thurs | Fri | Sat | Sun |
|---|---|---|---|---|---|---|---|
| Saying "Please" | | | | | | | |
| Saying "Thank You" | | | | | | | |
| Waiting Patiently | | | | | | | |
| Using "May I" | | | | | | | |
| Sharing | | | | | | | |

You can find full-page, customizable color incentive charts at www.mothersfriendsos.com. From *Enjoy the Ride* by Suzy Martyn ©2009. Permission granted to reproduce this page for personal use.

# Books and Websites

## Books:

***Babyhood*** by Paul Reiser (Avon Books, 1998)
> A funny and refreshing look at parenting from a dad's perspective.

***Be Brave, Anna*** by JoDee McConnaughhay (Happy Day Books, 1999)
> Practical tool for teaching your children to manage fear at bedtime.

***Because I Said So*** by John Rosemond (Andrews McMeel Publishing, 1996)
> Good 'Ol Fashioned Child-Rearing from a dad and psychologist who believes in natural (and some artificially created...) consequences to motivate children and change behavior.

***Creative Correction*** by Lisa Whelchel (Focus, 2005)
> Inspiring methods that encourage using scripture to back up discipline.

***Go Away Big Green Monster*** by Ed Emberley (Little, Brown and Company, 1992)
> Helps children feel more in control of those scary creatures that they might face at bedtime.

***Grandloving*** by Sue Johnson and Julie Carlson (Heartstrings Press, 2006)
Practical ideas for nurturing quality relationships between grandparents and grandchildren.

***How to Talk So Kids Will Listen & Listen So Kids Will Talk*** by Adele Faber and Elaine Mazlish (Collins Living, 1995)
Real-life situations and how to respond in ways that promote more talking and more listening.

***Toilet-Training in Less Than a Day*** by Nathan Azrin (Pocket, 1989)
Using a doll to teach potty-training to children at least 2.5 years old.

***Raising Great Kids*** and ***Boundaries with Kids*** by Henry Cloud and John Townsend (Zondervan, 2000 and 2001 respectively)
Down-to-earth philosophies that will inspire and equip.

***Siblings Without Rivalry*** by Adele Faber (Collins Living, 2004)
How to nurture the very important relationship between siblings and help avoid some of the most common problems between siblings.

***Spiritual Growth in Children*** by John Trent (Focus, 2003)
Includes very practical lists of spiritual stages, needs, readiness by ages.

***The Blessing*** by Gary Smalley and John Trent (Thomas Nelson, 2004)
The blessing that every child needs, especially from their earthly father.

***The New Read Aloud Handbook*** by Jim Trelease (Penguin, 2006)
The single most important thing you can do to prepare your child's reading readiness.

*The Secret Keeper Girl* (series) by Dannah Gresh (Moody Publishers, 2004)
> A series of dates for mom and pre-teen daughter to open up discussion on self-esteem and self-worth.

## Websites:

**www.mothersfriendsos.com**
Suzy Martyn's website with products, consulting, blog, tips, and much more

**www.disney.go.com**
games, videos, music, live events, parks, shop

**www.familyfun.go.com**
crafts, recipes, creative idea galore

**www.family.org**
Focus on the Family resources

**www.familyinternet.about.com**
basics, safety, education, projects

**www.flylady.net**
a practical way to get out of a life of chaos

**www.pbskids.org**
public television site

**www.scholastic.com**
for teachers, parents, administrators, librarians, and more

**www.tripadvisor.com**
reviews, tips, and information to plan family trips

**Enjoy the Ride**

**www.kids.yahoo.com**
games, movies, music, ecards, jokes

**www.familylife.com**
resources for healthy marriage

**www.momsintouch.org**
resources for moms who want to pray for their children at school

**www.pluggedinonline.com**
movie, TV, and game reviews

**www.aplaceofourown.org**
resources for daycare providers

**www.focusonyourchild.com**
part of focus on the family

**www.creativecorrection.com**
Lisa Welchel's site

**www.parenthacks.com**
practical tips on parenting

**www.parenting.com**
comprehensive parenting website

**www.ivillage.com**
comprehensive parenting website

**www.cdc.gov/vaccines/**
department of health and human services on vaccines and immuniza-
tions

**www.half.com**
books at half off!

# Index

# About the Author

For 25 years, **Suzy Martyn** has been caring for children in the classroom, in her home childcare, through her parenting consultation service, and with her three daughters. Serving as a keynote speaker for Babies "R" Us and Mothers of Preschoolers, she shares her knowledge and experience with parents all over southern California. Her advice has appeared in national parenting magazines, as well as in her monthly column "Parent Matters" for the Orange County Event News. Suzy holds a Masters in Education specializing in language acquisition, an Advanced Bachelor's degree in Liberal Studies, a Multiple Subject Teaching Credential, and a Language Development Certificate.

Visit www.mothersfriendsos.com to add your name to Suzy's email list, book speaking engagements, purchase books and other products, or for parenting consultation services. Email Suzy at suzy@mothersfriendsos.com.

## Parents, Teachers, and Caregivers:
## Invite Suzy Martyn to speak at your next event.

With warm wit and inspiring stories, Suzy equips her audiences to successfully manage the toughest challenges including:

- **Motivating picky eaters** to make healthful choices
- **Getting to the root of anger** in a child and helping manage it
- **Instilling a sense of responsibility** and a good work ethic
- **Setting limits** in firm, yet loving ways
- **Teaching your child the art of sleep** so you can get some rest
- **Potty-training your two-year-old** with simplicity and low stress
- **Motivating your children to joyfully get along**
- **Conquering your unique parenting challenges**

---

## Suzy provides personalized one-on-one coaching

She will walk with you through your unique situation so that you can meet your parenting goals and start to "Enjoy the Ride" of parenting.

## To invite Suzy to speak in your community, request personalized help, follow her blog, and read reviews, please visit:

Website: www.mothersfriendsos.com
E-mail: suzy@mothersfriendsos.com